CENTRE FOR EDUCATIONAL RESEARCH AND INNOVATION

WITHDRAWN
WRIGHT STATE UNIVERSITY LIBRARIES

Post-compulsory Education for Disabled People

ORGANISATION FOR ECONOMIC CO-OPERATION AND DEVELOPMENT

LC
4818.38
.P67
1997

ORGANISATION FOR ECONOMIC CO-OPERATION AND DEVELOPMENT

Pursuant to Article 1 of the Convention signed in Paris on 14th December 1960, and which came into force on 30th September 1961, the Organisation for Economic Co-operation and Development (OECD) shall promote policies designed:

- to achieve the highest sustainable economic growth and employment and a rising standard of living in Member countries, while maintaining financial stability, and thus to contribute to the development of the world economy;
- to contribute to sound economic expansion in Member as well as non-member countries in the process of economic development; and
- to contribute to the expansion of world trade on a multilateral, non-discriminatory basis in accordance with international obligations.

The original Member countries of the OECD are Austria, Belgium, Canada, Denmark, France, Germany, Greece, Iceland, Ireland, Italy, Luxembourg, the Netherlands, Norway, Portugal, Spain, Sweden, Switzerland, Turkey, the United Kingdom and the United States. The following countries became Members subsequently through accession at the dates indicated hereafter: Japan (28th April 1964), Finland (28th January 1969), Australia (7th June 1971), New Zealand (29th May 1973), Mexico (18th May 1994), the Czech Republic (21st December 1995), Hungary (7th May 1996), Poland (22nd November 1996) and the Republic of Korea (12th December 1996). The Commission of the European Communities takes part in the work of the OECD (Article 13 of the OECD Convention).

The Centre for Educational Research and Innovation was created in June 1968 by the Council of the Organisation for Economic Co-operation and Development and all Member countries of the OECD are participants.

The main objectives of the Centre are as follows:

- *to promote and support the development of research activities in education and undertake such research activities where appropriate;*
- *to promote and support pilot experiments with a view to introducing and testing innovations in the educational system;*
- *to promote the development of co-operation between Member countries in the field of educational research and innovation.*

The Centre functions within the Organisation for Economic Co-operation and Development in accordance with the decisions of the Council of the Organisation, under the authority of the Secretary-General. It is supervised by a Governing Board composed of one national expert in its field of competence from each of the countries participating in its programme of work.

Publié en français sous le titre :

L'ENSEIGNEMENT POST-OBLIGATOIRE POUR LES PERSONNES HANDICAPÉES

© OECD 1997
Permission to reproduce a portion of this work for non-commercial purposes or classroom use should be obtained through the Centre français d'exploitation du droit de copie (CFC), 20, rue des Grands-Augustins, 75006 Paris, France, Tel. (33-1) 44 07 47 70, Fax (33-1) 46 34 67 19, for every country except the United States. In the United States permission should be obtained through the Copyright Clearance Center, Customer Service, (508)750-8400, 222 Rosewood Drive, Danvers, MA 01923 USA, or CCC Online: http://www.copyright.com/. All other applications for permission to reproduce or translate all or part of this book should be made to OECD Publications, 2, rue André-Pascal, 75775 Paris Cedex 16, France.

FOREWORD

The enquiry leading to this document follows on from a project undertaken by the Centre for Educational Research and Innovation (CERI) of the OECD and reported in the 1995 OECD publication (*Integrating Students with Special Needs into Mainstream Schools*). It is one component of a further study of inclusive education being carried out by CERI over the period 1994 to 1997. The overall goal of the study is "to gather detailed information and data to inform governments and others on the implications of inclusive educational provision for the organisation of schools and services and their financing".

Whereas most of the study focuses on schools in selected countries, this particular component seeks to provide an overview of arrangements for educating and training people with disabilities once they pass beyond the age of compulsory schooling. It was prompted in part by current concerns across OECD countries about people's access to the labour market and about means of preparing them for it.

Twelve countries participated: Australia, Canada (British Columbia and Quebec), Finland, France, Iceland, Ireland, Italy, the Netherlands, Norway, Spain, Sweden and the United Kingdom. They provided reports and associated case studies in response to a questionnaire devised for the study's Steering Committee by a working group consisting of the director of the study, the study's senior consultant and country representatives from Norway, the United Kingdom and the United States. This document is based on the responses received.

Part 1 considers trends identified across participating countries with respect to prevalence of disabilities, related national policies and legislation, transition from schooling, funding, provision, the curriculum, support services, information technology, teacher training, community involvement, and eventual outcomes for people with disabilities. Achievements are summarised and aspects requiring further development are emphasised.

Part 2 presents key information derived from the country reports, under the same "issues" headings as those used in Part 1. Within each section the information is presented on a country by country basis, thus enabling readers both to gain some indication of the evidence base for the general trends identified and to follow developments in any one country.

The document was prepared by Don Labon with Peter Evans of the CERI Secretariat and is published on the responsibility of the Secretary-General of the OECD.

TABLE OF CONTENTS

SUMMARY

This document is one outcome of the 1994-1997 CERI study "Effective education and support structures for students with disabilities in integrated settings". Concerned with post-compulsory educational opportunities in 12 Member countries of the OECD for adolescents and adults with disabilities, it relies on information collected during 1995 and 1996 through responses to a detailed questionnaire and associated notes of guidance. The first part of the document confines itself to the main trends identified. The second part provides accounts of developments in the individual countries responding.

Policies in the participating countries recognise the needs of people with disabilities for post-compulsory education and training, and they all have some legislation in place to facilitate the implementation of these policies, but there is much variation in the extent to which this legislation protects people's rights. People with disabilities continue to be under-represented in post-compulsory education and in employment.

School leavers generally can have access to two or three years of further education, but take-up is lower among those with disabilities. In some cases, disabilities are compensated for by the allowance of extra time. Courses may be social, vocational or academic in form, and there is increasing emphasis on vocational courses. Some countries refer to the problem that many leave before completing their courses.

While access to higher education generally is conditional on performance on further education courses, in some cases special concessions are made for students with disabilities, on the basis that they have been under-performing academically. Traditional distinctions between academic and vocational courses are beginning to lessen, and the presence of the latter in higher education is increasing. There continue to be cases, however, where access for people with disabilities is limited unnecessarily, on the assumption that they will be unable to manage workshop activities.

Throughout the document, consideration of the prevalence of disabilities is made difficult by the fact that there are no consistent definitions across countries, not only of emotional and learning difficulties but also of apparently clear-cut entities such as auditory, visual and physical impairment. Even within an individual country, definitions can be inconsistent.

All the participating countries have arrangements for assessing students' achievements as they reach the end of compulsory education, but only some of those with disabilities have access to specialist advice. All the countries provide financial allowances for individuals with disabilities, and most help institutions meet the extra costs of providing for them, but the adequacy of these forms of funding varies considerably.

For those who do gain post-compulsory education and training places, modification of buildings to provide access is widespread, and there are various examples of extra teaching help, modified course materials and special computer resources. In most countries many of the institutions run their own counselling and welfare services and most have at least some access to external support services, some of which are provided by voluntary bodies. Evaluation of the effectiveness of course provision is rare, as is that of support services and of employment outcomes. Opportunities for specialist teacher training in this field tend to be limited.

Part 1

MAIN TRENDS

MAIN TRENDS

INTRODUCTION

This study of inclusive education takes place over the period 1995 to 1997 and follows on directly from a project considering developments in the integration of children with learning difficulties and disabilities within ordinary schools across the countries of the OECD as a whole. General trends were identified through consideration of individual country reports and common features of good practice were drawn out of an analysis of case studies. Findings were published by the OECD in 1995 in a book entitled *Integrating Students with Special Needs into Mainstream Schools*.

Most of this study consists of a more in-depth exploration of promising developments in a sample of schools in eight countries and a consideration of factors associated with their success. In addition, the study has three subsidiary components: one concerned with the training of teachers, one with multi-professional training and one, the one reported here, with post-compulsory education and training.

This consideration of post-compulsory education and training arose as an upward extension of the previous project, which was concerned only with children up to the end of their period of statutory schooling. The desirability of surveying developments for students with disabilities beyond the age of compulsory schooling was strengthened by current concerns across Member countries of the OECD with people's access to the labour market and with means of preparing them for it.

As with the previous project, the method of enquiry adopted for this component of the present study was a questionnaire leading to country reports and associated case studies. The objectives, scope and time scale of the enquiry were agreed upon at a meeting of the study's Steering Committee in September 1994.

Most participating countries needed extra time to prepare their reports, and the database from which this document is derived was accumulated by summer 1996. The reports vary considerably in detail, several lack statistical data sought and not all of the issues raised are addressed. Reports were received from Australia, the Canadian provinces of British Columbia and Quebec, Finland, France, Iceland, Ireland, Italy, the Netherlands, Norway, Spain, Sweden and the

United Kingdom. In the case of the United Kingdom, the arrangements referred to apply in England, where most of the kingdom's population reside, but not necessarily in Scotland, Northern Ireland or Wales.

In the following sections, the key questions put to Member countries are presented in bold italics.

A.   MAIN CHARACTERISTICS OF POST-COMPULSORY EDUCATION

What are the main characteristics of post-compulsory education and training in your country generally, in terms of structure, age range and goals?

In all the countries under consideration here, post-compulsory education and training opportunities exist for people of all ages beyond the statutory school leaving age, although most of them are aimed primarily at those in the 16 to 21 year age range. These opportunities can be divided broadly into *two levels*: at the lower level there is *further education* (FE), followed mostly by students in the 16 to 18 or 16- to 19-year age range, and at the upper level there is *higher education* (HE), taken up by some of these students, usually during the three years immediately following their participation in further education. Clarity of distinction between FE and HE varies appreciably from one country to another.

Cutting across this division into the levels of FE and HE is another broad division, that into *three types* of course: *social*, *vocational* and *academic*. As with FE and HE, the distinction between these types of course is not clear-cut.

Social courses are almost invariably at the level of FE. They may serve to train people for independent living or they may help them to develop leisure activities, and the former are of particular concern to a proportion of those with disabilities. People with disabilities, however, do not necessarily require social training, and they may participate in vocational or academic courses, both of which can occur either at the level of FE or at that of HE. Where academic courses are at the level of FE, they are often regarded as a form of preparation for HE, and entrance to HE is almost invariably conditional on the possession of qualifications at the FE level.

In the countries under consideration here, students having completed their compulsory schooling have a statutory right to either two or three years of FE. Take-up generally is high, of the order of 90 per cent or more of leavers from compulsory schooling in some cases. At its simplest, FE can consist of foundation courses preparing people for independent living or for training in basic crafts, or it can be a repetition of courses in subjects taken at school. At its most demanding, it can include training for advanced craft, technician and supervisor jobs, or an academic education sufficiently advanced to provide its successful examinees with eligibility for university entrance.

Among young people passing beyond the age range of compulsory schooling, while the proportion entering FE is high, the proportion leaving before the end of the first three years of post-compulsory education can also be significant. In Finland, for example, whereas 98 per cent of school leavers enter FE at 16, only 71 per cent of 16- to 19-year-olds are still in education. In Italy, 25 per cent of FE entrants leave within the first two years.

Within the field of FE, there is a lot of variation in the extent to which school leavers enter academic or vocational courses. Whereas some 80 per cent move on to academic courses in Ireland, only 32 per cent do so in Italy. There are signs of an increasing emphasis on vocational courses, related presumably to a reduction in traditional employment opportunities and countries' wishes to ensure that young people develop the new skills needed in a time of increasingly rapid technological change.

Among the different basic types of post-compulsory education and training, the greatest changes appear to be occurring in the field of vocational training, and it may be that traditional distinctions between academic and vocational courses are becoming blurred. In Australia, for example, vocational courses are becoming more flexible, linking increasingly both with industry and with academic courses, and appearing increasingly at levels of HE as well as of FE. The educational status of vocational training is also being raised in Spain, where there are current developments in higher vocational training and the likely future development of more vocationally-oriented degrees. In Australia and in the United Kingdom there are nationally recognised vocational qualifications.

B. THE POPULATION UNDER CONSIDERATION

Within the country's total population beyond the age of compulsory education, what percentage is currently considered to have one or more disabilities?

What degrees and kinds of disability are experienced by the people included in this percentage?

It should be pointed out that the population under consideration here is not simply an upward extension of the population of compulsory school age. Some children with disabilities will leave school not wishing to participate in any further education and indeed may not require it. If they do, the flexibility and diversity of post-school opportunities for education and training may be such that they can participate without requiring any adaptations to the curriculum on offer more generally. Moreover, some children recover from their disabilities, some do not survive to adulthood and some people acquire disabilities, for example through teenage motor accidents.

As had been found in the earlier project with respect to children (see *Integrating Students with Special Needs into Mainstream Schools*, OECD, 1995), definitions of disability with respect to people beyond the age range of compulsory education differ considerably from one country to another. Because of this, apparent differences between countries in the prevalence of disabilities are inevitably greater than those which really exist.

While countries such as Australia, Spain and the United Kingdom use the World Health Organisation's 1980 international classification, they do not necessarily use it consistently. In Australia, for example, there are regional variations in usage and it is not always clear to the Australian Bureau of Statistics which definition is being used in any given case. Other countries use very different criteria. In Norway, a distinction is made between educational disability and disability in relation to work, and in Italy the statistics for those with disabilities in post-compulsory education are based on the certification process through which children with special needs are deemed to have a right to extra educational help.

Given these kinds of difference in criteria used, it is hardly surprising that there are massive apparent differences in prevalence of disability. The examples in the following table, mostly referring to percentages with disabilities among adults generally, illustrate the point.

The age range from which statistics are drawn is a significant factor. For example, the Australian figures indicate that the prevalence of disability increases rapidly with age beyond 45. The Italian statistics refer only to the early years of post-compulsory education.

Country	Percentage with disabilities
Australia	18.0
Spain	15.0
United Kingdom	14.0
Norway	3.0
Italy	0.2

In the Netherlands, the problem of taking into account different levels of disability is recognised through a "triple trichotomy", whereby a third of the entire population in the age range 6 to 65 years is considered to have some kind of impairment or defect, a third of this group (some 11 per cent of the total) has a disability and a third of this sub-group (some 4 per cent of the total) has one or more severe disabilities.

Among those identified as having disabilities, the differences in proportions considered to have different types of disability also vary considerably from one country to another, and here too the apparent differences in percentages in any one category are probably largely attributable to differences in criteria for classification rather than to real differences.

Comparisons are further confounded by the fact that different countries have different kinds of category. The Italian report, for example, is the only one to use the composite category "psychophysical", into which 78 per cent of students with disabilities in further education are placed, and the Australian statistics differ from the rest in using the category of disability in manual dexterity, within which some 9 per cent of adults with disabilities are placed.

Even where the categories used appear similar, there are marked discrepancies between countries' figures. The Australian report identifies 21 per cent of adults with disabilities as having mobility problems, whereas the Spanish report indicates that 71 per cent of people with disabilities in the 18 to 64 age range have physical disabilities. The following table illustrates countries' different estimates of the prevalence of students with sensory disabilities as percentages of students with disabilities as a whole in post-compulsory education. The figures for Finland and Italy are for students in ordinary further education establishments and those for France relate to higher education.

Country	Auditory impairment (%)	Visual impairment (%)
Finland	1.5	0.5
France	15.0	19.0
Italy	15.0	7.0

In conclusion, the variations noted above point firmly to the need for common criteria in gathering educational statistics of this kind. To be meaningful and comparable, the figures for each country should reflect not only total prevalence of the various disabilities among different age groups but also prevalence of these disabilities in different levels and types of education. In gathering these statistics, it should be recognised that criteria referenced to employability or health would be likely to yield different results, relevant to different considerations.

C. POLICIES AND LEGISLATION

What international or national policies concerning post-compulsory education and training for people with disabilities are stated by the government of your country?

What arrangements exist for inter-agency collaboration to give effect to policies?

What national legislation governs, or provides advice or conditions concerning, post-compulsory education and training for people with disabilities?

Policy and policy development

Among the countries participating in the study there is a general recognition of the needs of people with disabilities for post-compulsory education and training, and this is reflected to varying degrees in countries' policy statements. These statements are commonly based on principles of normalisation and stress the rights of access for students with disabilities to provision designed for students generally.

Australia, Italy and the Nordic countries are particularly explicit about the rights of people with disabilities. In Australia, for example, there is active endorsement of the principle of "least restrictive environment" and stress on the unlawfulness of discrimination against people with disabilities. In Sweden, there is the expressed intention to go beyond simple financial compensation for disabilities towards ensuring that people with disabilities can use their assets to the full.

Despite countries' good intentions, people with disabilities continue to be under-represented in education and in employment. This is recognised in the countries most active in attempting to implement policies helpful to people with disabilities, where systematic enquiries concerning the effectiveness of these policies have been undertaken. It seems likely that this is also the case elsewhere.

Various examples can be cited of co-operation across departments, at national level, serving to assist in policy co-ordination that attempts to meet the needs of people with disabilities. Ireland, the Netherlands, Spain and the United Kingdom all have interdepartmental co-ordinating committees, with as many as 15 departments represented at meetings of the United Kingdom's co-ordination meetings, and in Italy there are strong links between the education, treasury and labour ministries. Some aspects of post-compulsory education may be run by departments other than that of education; in British Columbia, for example, the ministry of labour runs vocational rehabilitation programmes.

Other countries also recognise the need for increased co-operation. A recent enquiry in Finland, for example, concluded that while some inter-departmental collaboration occurred with respect to provision for people with disabilities, there was insufficient legislation to ensure that it occurred regularly.

Legislation

All the participating countries have some legislation in place to ensure that policies with respect to disabilities are implemented, but there is much variation in the extent to which people's needs are covered and there are various moves in the direction of further legislation to protect people's rights and give them access to post-compulsory education and training. In Nordic countries, for example, students have a statutory right to three years of further education after completion of compulsory schooling and in Italy most legislation concerned with assessment and provision for children with disabilities has been shifted upwards to also embrace students in further education.

Some of the legislation is particularly oriented towards helping young people, including those with disabilities, enter the labour market. In France, for example, all students leaving school without having passed the school leaving examination, which confers a certificate of professional aptitude, are entitled to further education designed to enhance their employability.

There is relatively little legislation specific to the needs of students with disabilities entering higher education, although some aspects are covered by more general legislation. This may include legislation designed to prevent people with disabilities being discriminated against, to provide them with equipment and with transport services, and to ensure that they have access to public buildings.

D. TRANSITION FROM SCHOOLING

Prior to school leaving, what forms of assessment are undertaken to determine the kinds of post-compulsory education and training that might be suitable for students with disabilities?

What arrangements exist in schools to facilitate the transition of students with disabilities from school to some form of post-compulsory education and training?

All participating countries have arrangements for assessing pupils' achievements as they reach the end of compulsory schooling and for helping them consider their further education, training and employment prospects. Specialist assessment and advice facilities for those with special needs exist generally but not all young people with disabilities have access to them. Countries vary considerably in the depth of assessment and advice offered. They also vary in the relative emphases they place on within-school and outside-school resources, with the more well developed services consisting of a judicious mixture of the two.

The Australian report refers to comprehensive arrangements through which young people with disabilities are advised on post-school options, although these arrangements are not mandatory and survey findings indicate that only about half the target population have access to them. Transition planning contributes to a whole life plan, through which teachers tailor the curriculum to meet individual needs, assess performance and contribute to the work of transition planning teams which also include the young people themselves, their parents and representatives of relevant agencies. Outcomes include an agreed set of goals for each student involved.

Similar arrangements exist, for the relatively small proportions of the age groups formally assessed as having disabilities, in Italy and in the United Kingdom. In these two countries there is the advantage that the procedures are mandatory, with multi-disciplinary reviews of progress occurring annually. In the United Kingdom, there is a particular stress on the involvement of parents as partners in the review process. Legislation in Spain also calls for a comprehensive system of guidance for all school leavers, including the setting of educational and vocational objectives, but resources have not as yet been developed sufficiently in schools for this to be in place generally.

Continuity from compulsory to post-compulsory education for young people with special needs is helped in Ireland by the fact that the final years of the former and the early part of the latter occur in the same establishment. In Finland, where advice is strongly school-based, continuity is helped by the fact that secondary school staff have a duty to continue to provide some support for the young people they have taught after these former pupils have reached the end of compulsory schooling and have therefore moved on.

Advice is also strongly school-based in Sweden, where each school has a member of staff responsible for further educational and vocational guidance, but in relation to young people with disabilities staff can also call on municipality-based advisers with relevant expertise who are funded in part by the Swedish Agency for Special Education.

In Norway on the other hand, guidance is to a greater extent the province of educational psychologists, who assess school leavers, co-ordinate relevant information, liaise with further education establishments and advise admissions boards as to whether individual applicants should be accorded priority on the basis of disability.

E.   FUNDING

What funding, from which sources, is available to support the various forms of post-compulsory education and training for people with disabilities?

Two kinds of funding are reported. One is the provision of money to institutions providing for people with disabilities, and the other is the provision of money, equipment or services directly to the people with disabilities or to the individuals looking after them. Almost all the participating countries provide some form of extra funding to institutions, and this is generally determined at national level, though it may be administered locally.

All the countries offer some help to individuals, usually according to national criteria with some local monitoring, but the extent to which individuals have access to such help is not altogether clear from the reports received. While most of the funding comes from the state, some comes from sources such as religious bodies, the European Social Fund, and voluntary organisations concerned with particular disabilities.

Funds provided to institutions may be in the form of one-off grants for particular purposes, for example for the modification of buildings to enable students with disabilities to gain physical access to teaching areas, or they may be on a recurrent basis to allow for the continuing extra costs of providing the students with appropriate tuition.

Such funds may be channelled through particular institutions rather than be provided as a matter of course to all. In Quebec, for example, two colleges designated as centres of excellence with respect to provision for disabilities receive government funding to enable them to service all the colleges in the province, offering facilities such as escorts and specialised teaching materials. Similar arrangements exist in British Columbia.

Institutions may receive government or municipal funds on the assumption that a proportion of their students will have disabilities or the money may be targeted more precisely, in accordance with the enrolment of identified individuals. In Norway, for example, enterprises taking on apprentices with disabilities can receive an allowance per apprentice of up to three times the standard allowance, if extra training costs can be demonstrated. In the United Kingdom, parts of the extra allowances given to further education institutions and to commercial organisations running vocational training schemes are conditional upon the achievement of goals that are agreed at the start of each programme.

A key consideration is the extent to which funding to institutions for individuals with disabilities is administered in such a way as to encourage integration or segregation. Finland is a country which seems to have managed to achieve a system that is fairly neutral in this respect. Whereas the "ordinary" student counts as a unit of 1.0 for funding purposes, someone with a disability counts as 1.5, whether that person is enrolled in a mainstream institution or in a special education institution. In special education institutions, however, any student recognised as having a severe disability counts as 2.25.

While the extent to which individuals can claim disability allowances varies from one country to another, the items on which they are spent are very similar. Country reports refer to adaptation of housing, escorting, home help, interpreting through signing, special equipment, teaching programmes, transliteration of texts, and transport. An Australian estimate referred to the extra cost per annum per student as being greatest for visual impairment and least, at less than a third of this, for intellectual disability.

However, the provision of services is not necessarily without constraints. In Ireland, for example, there are university grants covering tuition and transport which are available for students with disabilities. In practice, these students are treated more generously than other students with special needs who would also benefit from additional support. Some services, home help in Sweden for example, are subject to means testing.

F. PROVISION

Taking the group of people with disabilities at post-compulsory education age levels nationally, what percentage of this group receives one or other form of education and training?

What numbers are involved at various age levels? What conditions did these people have to meet in order to enter these forms of education and/or training?

In your view, how many people with disabilities who are eligible for post-compulsory education and/or training, and who could benefit from it, do not receive it?

How effective are existing arrangements to identify and assess any special needs among enrolled students generally?

Comparisons across countries of the proportions of pupils with disabilities leaving compulsory education and continuing into some form of post-compulsory education or training are difficult to make, partly because not all the countries gather the relevant statistics and partly because when they do their criteria for defining disability may vary. It is clear, however, that actual percentages vary too.

In Australia, on the one hand, whereas over 70 per cent of school leavers continue in education or enter training schemes, among those with disabilities only about a quarter do so. In the Netherlands, among people aged 18 to 45, the proportion of those with disabilities having achieved a secondary or higher level of education is only about half that in the age range as a whole, and among those leaving special schools 28 per cent do not continue into post-compulsory education. In Iceland and in Norway on the other hand, almost all school leavers with disabilities move on to some form of further education or training.

In some cases pupils with disabilities stay on at school beyond school leaving age. In Finland, for example, whereas only 8 per cent of the cohort as a whole stay on, almost a third of those with disabilities do so. Most of the special schools in Ireland have places for students of up to three years beyond the age range of compulsory schooling. In the Netherlands, students can continue in special schools to the age of 20 years, or more in exceptional cases.

Even when students with disabilities do undertake post-compulsory education or training, they do not necessarily complete the courses for which they have enrolled. In Finland, results of a survey of school leavers with emotional and behavioural difficulties indicated that almost half of the 70 per cent going on to further education dropped out. In Norway, similarly, it was found that only 20 per cent of further education entrants with disabilities completed the full three years.

In order to encourage take-up of post-compulsory education and training opportunities among people with disabilities, and as a means of helping to compensate them for aspects of disability, in several countries usual entry requirements are waived.

In Australia, for example, higher education courses run on a distance learning basis have open access. In Ireland, some higher education establishments grant special interviews to students with disabilities who may have underperformed in examinations. Students with disabilities can enter higher education establishments in Norway without their having to meet conventional entrance requirements. In the United Kingdom, people with disabilities do not have to satisfy the general requirement of being unemployed for six months before starting on a training for work scheme.

The majority of further education entrants with disabilities appear to be placed on vocational training courses in mainstream establishments. It is not altogether clear from the country reports, however, whether these are generally the most appropriate placements for them or whether the placements are the outcomes of detailed assessment.

In some cases it is evident that detailed assessments are being undertaken. The tailoring of placements to suit individual students' assessed aptitudes is referred to as being practised fairly widely in the report from Australia. Extensive assessment arrangements are available in Ireland to students with disabilities who have completed a period of further education. In the United Kingdom, most further education institutions have introduced screening procedures to identify the students who will need help in developing the literacy and numeracy skills required for successful course completion. In Quebec, students with disabilities can only be refused admission to ordinary classes if the colleges can demonstrate beyond all doubt that they are unable to make the necessary adaptations.

Placement of a significant proportion of school leavers with disabilities in special classes or centres was referred to in reports from Finland, France, Iceland, Ireland, Norway and Sweden. The extent to which these placements are appropriate is not altogether clear.

G.   THE CURRICULUM

Within each post-compulsory sector (i.e. in higher, in vocational, in social, or in any other form of education and/or training), what programmes are available to students with disabilities?

Are there any other programmes that are available to students generally and that could be of benefit to students with disabilities but that are not accessible to them? If so, what are they, why are they not accessible and how could they be made so?

In relation to the programmes available to students with disabilities, and as means of ensuring their appropriate education and training, what modifications are made: to buildings; to teaching areas; to curriculum content; to learning materials; to teaching methods; to assessment procedures?

To what extent do these modifications meet the educational and training needs of people with disabilities?

To what extent are the programmes on offer evaluated, in relation to students with disabilities, either by the establishments themselves or by individuals or organisations external to these establishments?

How well designed are these evaluations? What are their results?

Across the participant countries, the programmes available to students with disabilities are in principle all the programmes available to students generally. In practice, because of their perceived limitations, which are not always real, students with disabilities tend to be enrolled for certain types of vocational or social training course. In Norway, for example, only 7 per cent of students with disabilities in further education take academic courses. In Finland, the vocational courses in which students with disabilities are most commonly enrolled are in home economics, cooking, cleaning, metalwork, vehicle maintenance and building construction. Special classes in Ireland focus on communication skills, numeracy, social development and health education.

Even when students with disabilities follow academic courses, certain types of course tend to predominate. In Quebec, for example, students with disabilities tend to follow courses in social sciences and in administration rather than in the natural sciences.

In some countries, some of the institutions providing courses for students generally have extra resources to enable them to ensure that they can offer a full range of courses to students with disabilities. Arrangements of this kind occur in British Columbia and Quebec. In Norway, two of the universities provide special services for students with disabilities and there is a teacher training course specially designed for trainee teachers with hearing impairment.

The report from Ireland refers to some students with sensory or motor disabilities being excluded from practical subjects, sometimes as a result of over-caution rather than of real hazard, and it seems quite likely that this occurs in other countries too. In the United Kingdom, students with disabilities are thought to be particularly under-represented in science programmes and on initial teacher training courses.

Widespread attempts to modify buildings to ensure that students with disabilities have access to the buildings themselves and to teaching areas within them are referred to in the reports from Australia, British Columbia, Quebec, Ireland and Norway. References are made to adaptations providing physical access through ramps and handrails, sensory access through tactile signs and audio cues, and communication access through pictorial signs. In Quebec, Finland, Ireland and Norway, building regulations require all new public buildings to provide physical access for people with disabilities.

Access to ordinary courses can be enhanced by providing escorts for people with physical disability or visual impairment, interpreters for people with hearing impairment or other difficulties with spoken language, and additional help from tutors for people with learning difficulties. Assistance of this kind occurs to some extent across participating countries generally and appears to be relatively extensive in Quebec, Iceland and Italy. Whereas team teaching was formerly used in Finland with classes including students with disabilities, as a result of recent funding restrictions this second teacher facility has been withdrawn.

The teaching materials used in ordinary courses can be modified by transliterating text into Braille or through computers which mediate between spoken and written language. Students' difficulties in speaking, writing, drawing and undertaking experimental work can be compensated for by computers and by various other technological and prosthetic aids. While instances of curriculum modification through adapted teaching materials or the use of special equipment occur in all participating countries, the extent to which people with disabilities have access to these facilities is not clear, and it may well vary markedly from one country to another.

Modifications to courses include providing additional beginner classes, reducing the number of subjects taken, selecting relevant modules, revising goals, adjusting duration, facilitating home study, changing teaching strategies and altering assessment methods. By means such as these, students with disabilities in Finland, for example, are able to obtain the same qualifications as do other students in the curriculum areas of catering, media, seafaring, social services, technology and health care. In other areas, there may be some modification in the qualification obtained. In Italy and in Norway there is particular stress on the development of individual education programmes, usually followed in ordinary classes.

There do not appear to be many nationally co-ordinated attempts to evaluate the success of institutions' procedures for enhancing access for people with disabilities to post-compulsory education and training programmes. Such evaluation as does occur seems have been largely that planned through initiatives of individuals in a few institutions.

While evaluation of provision for people with disabilities does not feature strongly in the country reports, there are some examples. In Finland, there is an annual follow-up of the use of funds allocated nationally to special education, and arrangements are being made to train staff in institutional self-assessment. National surveys seeking the opinions of teachers in further education concerning the suitability for students with disabilities of programmes, teaching help and technical aids have been conducted in Norway. In the United Kingdom, where the quality of further and higher education courses is assessed nationally, findings indicate that teachers in further education institutions are strongly committed to providing for students with disabilities but undertake little systematic analysis of what these students need.

H. SUPPORT SERVICES

Within the establishments under consideration, what support services are there to meet the educational, training or welfare needs of students with disabilities? What other relevant support services, based outside these establishments, are there?

To what extent are these internal and external support services appropriate and effective?

To what extent is there effective consultation across support services responsible to different agencies? To what extent are these support services evaluated, either within the establishments themselves or by individuals or organisations external to these establishments? How well designed are these evaluations? What are their results?

As young people pass beyond compulsory school age they become more likely to be in need of welfare and counselling support in their own right, rather than as members of families. Across the participating countries, further education establishments run their own support services for students generally, including those with disabilities. Services may include liaising with the community, providing information booklets, managing special entry and assessment arrangements, monitoring access to courses, mentoring, counselling, and helping students gain access to personal assistance and special teaching materials and equipment.

Reports from Australia, British Columbia, Finland, Iceland, Ireland, Italy and the United Kingdom indicate that most if not all of their further education establishments provide at least some of these services. In Finland these services have been reduced in recent years as a result of expenditure cuts in education generally. Higher education establishments also provide such services, although the reports from British Columbia and Italy indicate that there they are less extensive in universities than in further education, and this could also be the case in other countries.

The report from Finland refers to special vocational education establishments as offering more extensive support services than establishments providing primarily for students without disabilities. They recruit nationally, are concerned with particular disabilities, can advise other establishments, and liaise with national bodies concerned with disabilities.

Most further education establishments also have access to external support services, some of which are run by municipalities and some of which operate at regional or national level. Further education establishments in Finland, Ireland, Italy, Norway and the United Kingdom, for example, have access to their local medical, psychological and social services. Across the participant countries, voluntary bodies, often concerned with particular disabilities, run national and local services. The report from Spain indicates that people in large cities are rather better served by these facilities than are those in rural areas.

Services running at national level include the Tertiary Education Disability Council of Australia, which publishes a newsletter, runs conferences and collates information about the costs of providing services. Also in Australia, there is a scheme whereby regional disability liaison officers advise and consult with the officers appointed to individual further and higher education establishments in their regions. British Columbia's province-wide Vocational Rehabilitation Services arrange assessment, training, allowances, books, equipment and vehicle modification. In the United Kingdom the National Advisory Council on the Employment of People with Disabilities carries training as part of its brief.

Iceland has centres which, collectively, offer sign language interpretation, literacy courses, special materials and equipment, and computer aids. Similar services are offered in Ireland by the National Rehabilitation Board and in Norway by the country's 20 national resource centres for special education. The Swedish Agency for Special Education has 27 regional bases and provides a range of specialist advisory services.

The general pattern across participating countries is that of a plethora of services, some run within establishments and some run by local, regional or national public services, commercial organisations or voluntary bodies. There is little indication from the reports, however, either of the quality of these services or of the extent to which individuals with disabilities have access to them. Nor is there much indication as to the extent to which different services collaborate. 25

The United Kingdom appears to be exceptional in its systematic monitoring of support services run within further education institutions, where inspectors found in-college resource centres to be good at meeting students' physical needs but lacking specific objectives and linking insufficiently with mainstream courses. Norway is also exceptional in that there have been notable attempts there to co-ordinate education, health and welfare services.

I. INFORMATION TECHNOLOGY

Currently, to what extent are developments in information technology proving advantageous in the education and training of people with disabilities?

In the near future, what further educational and training benefits is information technology likely to make possible for people with disabilities?

Computers are in general use in post-compulsory education and training establishments across the participant countries. The existence of training programmes in the use of computers and of software developed for use by students with disabilities is widespread. The presence of national or regional centres developing special materials and equipment for distribution to people with disabilities is referred to in reports from Australia, Canada, Finland, Iceland, Norway, Spain, Sweden and the United Kingdom.

Facilities referred to as being generally available in one or more of these countries include automatic page turners, Braille computer terminals, equipment for converting between speech, text and Braille, ergonomic furniture, print enhancers, speech synthesisers, talking book machines, and talking typewriters.

Various facilities of interest are referred to in individual country reports. British Columbia has a province-wide service enabling people with disabilities to identify the technological skills they need to achieve their vocational goals, to borrow adaptive technology and software, to receive training in their use, and to have their borrowed equipment maintained and repaired. In Spain there is a computer-aided training programme in speech therapy.

In Finland, multimedia teaching programmes for students with disabilities are being produced. In Norway, a national database to catalogue existing special education software is being created. In the United Kingdom a database provides a forum through which support workers can discuss possible information technology solutions to learning problems experienced by their clients with disabilities.

In Australia a very extensive system useful for students generally and of particular use to students with mobility difficulties includes the design and development of educational resource materials, the broadcasting of courses by satellite and the running of an associated library network. Another Australian outreach system operates through the Internet and helps students with disabilities to use electronic mail to link with one another and with staff in further and higher education establishments.

While countries are at different stages in developing information technology services for the benefit of students with disabilities, as innovation in this field is rapid and as costs of particular facilities are falling, the more advanced facilities already available to some are likely to become much more widespread over the next few years. Future developments envisaged in country reports include tele-communications platforms which will make possible the integration of services such as recorded television programmes on demand, face to face tutorials, group conferencing, electronic mail and electronic library resources.

J.   TEACHER TRAINING

To what extent do teachers working in the post-compulsory education and training fields themselves receive initial or in-service training in teaching people with disabilities? How effective is this training?

Across the participant countries, as far as teachers in further and higher education generally are concerned the overall features are that training in teaching students with disabilities is not a requirement upon them and that few have expertise in this field, which suffers rather more neglect in higher education than in further education.

There are, however, some exceptions. The majority of further and higher education teachers in Australia and in the Canadian provinces of British Columbia and Quebec are involved in at least an element of relevant in-service training, mostly designed simply to raise their awareness of the issues involved but sometimes extending to workshops considering teaching methods. In Australia there is also a nationally available training kit focusing on teaching students with disabilities.

There is more substantial involvement of teachers generally in Finland, where individual differences are considered throughout initial training to teach on vocational courses. In Iceland and in Sweden, initial training includes a special education element for all. More than half the teachers in upper secondary schools in Norway have undertaken training of a year or more in special education.

Among teachers working primarily with students and trainees with disabilities, in most of the participant countries the proportion who have undertaken extensive specialist initial or in-service training does not appear to be known. The opportunities for such training do exist generally, however, often in the form of degree or diploma courses run in higher education establishments. In Finland, for example, teachers undertaking in-service training specifically to teach students with disabilities on vocational courses follow personal development plans in which the individualisation of teaching often features strongly.

In addition to the more extensive courses, there are various short-term courses, some of which count as modules towards higher education qualifications. In general, though, the availability of specialist training relevant to the teaching of students with disabilities in the post-compulsory sector appears to be less than that relating to work with those of compulsory school age.

Italy provides an exception to the general trend in that here all further education teachers working primarily with students who have certificates indicating special educational need are expected to undertake substantial specialist training. This is organised at regional level, is monitored by the country's Inspectorate, is taken over a two year period and consists largely of on-the-job training. The teacher carries out support teaching, mostly in ordinary classes, training includes studies of psychology and teaching methods, and qualification is contingent on successful completion of a thesis.

K. COMMUNITY INVOLVEMENT

Additional to the support services already referred to, are there any other noteworthy forms of community involvement enhancing post-compulsory education and training for people with disabilities? In what ways are they noteworthy?

Are members of the community generally helped to understand and meet needs for post-compulsory education and training among people with disabilities? If so, to what extent, by what means and how successfully?

In most participating countries, voluntary bodies are actively involved in issues concerning the further education of students with disabilities. In all these countries, the voluntary bodies are generally concerned with particular disabilities and they tend to be run by members of families in which there is a person with a disability.

Some of the reports refer to voluntary bodies concerned with disabilities as being particularly active. In Ireland, for example, they provide advice about available services and equipment, run conferences, and advocate particular kinds of treatment. In Norway, with financial support from the government, they are said to make an important supplementary contribution to public sector education and training. In Spain, they take a lead in involving the community more generally in disability considerations.

Unlike the majority of the reports, that from Finland indicates that the kinds of home-school links commonly found there in the phase of compulsory education do not continue into vocational education, and that voluntary work makes little contribution to further education generally.

Various examples are given of government and institutional initiatives designed to secure wider community involvement in the further education of students with disabilities. National initiatives in Australia have provided the basis for many partnerships between schools, vocational training establishments and industry. In Italy, parents are represented on the provincial and district councils for further education as well as on the councils of the further education institutions themselves.

In the United Kingdom, colleges of further education are particularly active in identifying and responding to local needs, as part of their processes of drawing up strategic plans, which are required from them by their national funding council. Each of the funding council's nine regional committees has several community representatives, including at least one with a special interest in the education of people with disabilities.

L.   POST-EDUCATION EXPERIENCE

How effective are the forms of post-compulsory education and training outlined here in enabling people with disabilities to become more independent, in preparing them for the labour market and in helping them make the most of their opportunities for leisure?

The answers to these questions do not appear to be known in any detail. While the report from Quebec refers to post-compulsory education as demonstrably reducing the later dependence among people with disabilities on social assistance schemes, among participant countries as a whole the general consensus is that they remain disadvantaged.

The report from Finland, for example, refers to people with disabilities as having particularly great difficulties in finding employment after vocational training. In the Netherlands it is estimated that at least 50 per cent of the students with impairments not completing secondary education will never find jobs. The report from Spain, while acknowledging much progress over the past 15 years, refers to the quality of life for people with disabilities as still being far from what it should be.

Only two country reports provide statistics putting employment prospects for students with disabilities leaving post-compulsory education into context. The unemployment rate among students with disabilities graduating from an Australian university was found to be twice that among the cohort of students generally. In a United Kingdom study, while the percentage of those with disabilities gaining a qualification was on a par with that pertaining generally, the percentage finding work was only just over three quarters that found among the whole group.

Strong evidence concerning quality of life among people with disabilities has emerged from surveys undertaken in Norway. By comparison with those without disabilities they are likely to participate less in working life, they are more likely to leave jobs through lack of suitable conditions, they take more sick leave, their educational attainments are lower, their incomes are lower, they often live alone or with their parents, they have higher living expenses, and they have difficulties in joining clubs and in participating in open air activities.

Strategies adopted by some governments to counteract these disadvantages include arranging sheltered work on an unpaid basis, encouraging staff in institutions to follow their trainees through into employment to help them adjust, subsidising employers, and having quota arrangements whereby employers are under some obligation to take on a certain proportion of people with disabilities.

M. WAYS FORWARD

Overall, what are the most promising developments and what more do you think should be done?

It is clear that participant countries differ considerably in the stages they have reached in developing post-compulsory education and training arrangements for people with disabilities, and that something fully achieved in one country may be no more than a distant aspiration in another. Countries' achievements in this field, however, are more appropriately viewed in the context of their own achievements in education generally, rather than in terms of cross-country comparisons.

While participant countries differ in what they have actually achieved, they exhibit a strong consensus in their views as to what can and should be done, given the resources needed. In other words, they are all travelling along broadly the same route. Developments in recent years, considered promising in one or more countries, include the following:

- The strategy of linking funding to establishments with requirements that they declare teaching objectives and outcomes has been highly successful.
- There has been progress with respect to further and higher education institutions' entrance requirements for students with disabilities.
- Participation rates for students and trainees with disabilities have increased, particularly in vocational training.
- Teachers' attitudes, teaching methods and approaches to assessment have improved.
- The development of regional and national resource centres has been of value.
- Considerable gains have been made through the use of technological resources.

Various developments are thought still to be needed, and an aggregated list of such developments, each referred to in at least one country report, inevitably echoes some of the items presented in the above list of achievements. The following can be placed on the agenda for change:

- There is a need for improved inter-agency collaboration.

- Arrangements to enhance transition from one stage of education and training to the next are in need of improvement.

- Disability allowances appear not to cover costs and should be reviewed with a view to individual targeting.

- The costs of assessment needed to provide documentary evidence of disability should be reduced.

- Participation rates for students and trainees with disabilities need to improve further.

- Establishments increasingly providing inclusive education and training for people with disabilities need continuing encouragement if they are to sustain their commitment.

- Vocational training for people with disabilities needs to be broadened, to become more versatile, and to be linked more closely with working life.

- Establishments should be more active in evaluating their provision for people with disabilities and in monitoring their effectiveness.

- With respect to disability issues there should be national codes of practice, accompanied by related staff development programmes, including reference to admission requirements, attitudes, teaching methods and assessment of students' progress.

- Support services within educational and training establishments should be improved, particularly in universities.

- Networking arrangements across institutions could help in the dissemination of expertise.

- Resource centres should clarify their roles and market their services more effectively.

- Technological resources should be developed further, within a policy framework, and the provision of technical aids should be co-ordinated more effectively.

- A systematic approach is needed to the effective training of all teachers who work with students and trainees with disabilities, with particular attention paid to the design and evaluation of individual teaching programmes.

CONCLUSION

Each of the issues addressed in this report provides examples of good practice, but they tend to occur in a minority of cases only. Quantification of data has proved difficult, as the country reports on which this account is based vary considerably in detail, several do not include statistical data sought and some lack responses to one or more of the clusters of questions asked.

It may well be that the governments concerned do not have access to this kind of information. If so, they are not yet in a position to assess developments in this field in any detail, and thus are unable to plan effectively for change. The questions asked here can provide cues to the areas which governments may choose to investigate.

One key area for further investigation is that of assessing the size and nature of the population under consideration. It is evident from the presentations of data concerning the prevalence of different types of disability that the criteria used to define disabilities differ considerably from one country to another. If international progress in this field is to be assessed effectively, it is essential that countries arrive at common definitions of disabilities. An OECD project designed to address this issue has been commissioned and is currently in the planning stage.

Another main area which appears to be insufficiently charted is the extent to which people with disabilities have appropriate opportunities for suitable post-compulsory education, training and employment. These opportunities can be enhanced by legislation which confirms the rights of people with disabilities to be treated equitably and encouraged to make full use of their assets. They can also be enhanced if individual disability allowances are realistic and if people with disabilities have full access to them, if institutions' entry requirements are appropriate, and if funding to institutions takes full account of the needs that students with disabilities have for support services.

Improvements in provision can only be effective if the attitudes and skills of the providers are appropriate, and it is clear that there is still much to be done both in the training of teachers generally in the field of post-compulsory education and in the further development of knowledge and skills among those choosing to specialise in this field. Furthermore, it is for the establishments themselves to take active steps to evaluate the comprehensiveness and effectiveness of their own provision. While they do not generally do this, there are isolated indications that government initiatives can be valuable in stimulating such developments.

While for many countries these agendas for change can be daunting, both in terms of the effort required and in terms of their costs, the latter are not necessarily as great as they may at first appear. If the outcomes are measurable in terms of people's increased independence and of the fulfilment of their potential as contributors to the economy, existing elements of public expenditure may be saved.

Part 2

SYNTHESIS OF COUNTRY REPORTS

INTRODUCTION

In this second part of the document key information derived from the country reports is presented, under the same "issues" headings as those used in the first part. Within each section the information is presented on a country by country basis. This should enable the reader both to gain some indication of the evidence base for the general trends identified and to follow developments in any one country. The notes of guidance which accompanied the key questions to Member countries are presented in Annex 2.

A. MAIN CHARACTERISTICS OF POST-COMPULSORY EDUCATION

Historically, **Australian** post-compulsory education has been separated into academic and vocational education, with academic education at the further education (FE) level taking place in senior secondary schools and leading into higher education (HE), and with vocational education remaining at the FE level and occurring in technical schools, technical and FE colleges, private colleges, and the workplace.

In recent years there has been increased emphasis in Australia on collaboration between education and industry in order to meet industry's rapidly evolving needs for skills and to improve training for people under-represented in the labour market. Vocational training is now more flexible, including elements of self-paced learning and distance learning. While managed regionally and locally, it is based on national competency standards and is set within a national qualification framework.

The traditional separation between vocational education and HE in Australia is being reduced considerably, with the fact that universities are funded nationally serving as a lever for change. Encouraged by the government to do so, universities are co-operating with the technical and FE colleges and with other providers of vocational education to share resources, run joint programmes and operate credit transfer systems.

Among people of post-compulsory age in **Finland** in 1990, students comprised 71 per cent of the 16 to 19 year age group, 32 per cent of those aged 20 to 24, 14 per cent of those aged 25 to 29 and 5 per cent of those aged 30 to 39. About

101 000 were in full-time senior secondary schools and 161 000 in full-time vocational institutions, with both kinds of establishment mostly run by the state or by the municipalities. Almost 252 000 were in other kinds of vocational training establishment, often attended on a fairly short-term basis and often run by commercial enterprises. Some 6 000 were taking social training courses in folk high schools and 7 000 were in apprenticeships.

In 1993, 98 per cent of comprehensive school leavers in Finland went on to FE, 55 per cent of them to senior secondary schools and 45 per cent to vocational institutions. Students may move on to HE either following senior secondary schooling or following vocational training.

From the late nineteenth century onwards, **Iceland** has had a variety of FE establishments, including vocational schools providing training for skilled trades, schools for domestic science, colleges for agriculture, commerce, marine engineering, nursing and art, and grammar schools preparing students for university entrance. Over the past 20 years most of these establishments have been replaced by upper secondary schools, now attended by 86 per cent of those passing the statutory school leaving age, operating largely on a unit-credit system and offering both vocational and academic courses.

Higher education in Iceland is undertaken mainly either in universities or in a variety of vocational, technical and art colleges. Postgraduate education is provided only within the university sector. Some establishments run both FE and HE courses.

In **Ireland**, compulsory schooling ends at 15 years and most pupils take the Junior Certificate Examination in their final compulsory year, but some students with disabilities do not take it until they are older. Compulsory education can be completed in secondary schools, vocational schools and colleges, comprehensive and community schools, or special schools, all overseen and supported financially by the Department of education and all following courses approved by the Department.

These Irish establishments also run two-year or three-year post-compulsory education courses known as senior cycle courses, which do not have entrance requirements, which lead to academic type or vocational type leaving certificates. All 15-year-olds are entitled to three years of post-compulsory education, almost all enter it, and about 80 per cent of entrants follow academic courses. Some establishments also provide adult literacy programmes and social programmes which teenagers and adults can follow, for example if they wish to develop hobbies.

As part of Ireland's FE there are also other vocational programmes, apprenticeship programmes in areas such as engineering and printing, training for work in tourism, a Youth reach programme for young people who have left school without formal qualifications, and vocational training opportunities for adults who have been unemployed for a long time. Higher education occurs in universities, teacher training colleges and technical colleges.

With compulsory education in **Italy** extending from 6 to 14 years, FE provision in the country's upper secondary schools caters largely for students in the 14 to 19 age range, although 25 per cent of entrants leave within the first two years. The schools have their own specialisms. In 1993, 31.6 per cent of entrants were to classical and scientific education, 3.5 per cent artistic, 35.8 per cent technical and 19.5 per cent vocational. Some schools specialise in individual vocational fields, such as catering, nursery school teaching, social work or tourism.

In the **Netherlands**, following three years of secondary education in which all children in ordinary schools follow the same basic education curriculum consisting of 15 subjects, the students divide out into different branches of senior secondary education, all of which continue beyond the compulsory education phase into FE provision. These branches offer a choice of general education, vocational education, and pre-university education. For those gaining entry to HE, it may take the form of higher vocational education, university education, or enrolment at the Open University.

Dating from the beginning of 1996, there has been in the Netherlands a fairly rapid development of regional education centres, with 24 approved by March 1996 and about 50 envisaged eventually across the country. The purpose of these centres is to co-ordinate vocational education offered by schools, day-release apprenticeship training systems and institutes for adults, and it is planned that eventually every regional education centre will offer the full range of educational provision at FE level for students aged 16 and over.

In **Norway**, FE is provided largely in upper secondary schools. Only 7 per cent of upper secondary school entrants enter wholly academic courses; 42 per cent take technical and industrial subjects, 13 per cent take domestic science, 11 per cent take commercial and clerical subjects, and most of the remainder study in areas such as health and social services, applied arts, agriculture and fishing.

At the level of FE, the **Spanish** system has traditionally maintained a particularly clear distinction between vocational and academic courses, with only the latter leading to HE. Since 1990, however, with the passing of the law of General Regulation of the Educational System, this is beginning to be replaced by a system whereby the traditional academic courses (for the *Baccalaureate*) at the level of FE run in parallel with intermediate vocational training courses. Both sets of courses will be able to lead either into conventional academic HE or into a form of HE known as higher vocational training.

37

It is still the case in Spain that almost the whole of HE is academic and university-based, although the future implementation of the country's recently introduced University Reform Act is likely to lead to the development of more vocationally-oriented degrees.

Beyond compulsory school age, all **Swedish** municipalities are required by law to offer free schooling in upper secondary schools to young people up to the age of 20. Upper secondary schools also run adult education courses. More than 90 per cent of compulsory school leavers enter and almost 90 per cent of entrants complete their courses within four years.

In Swedish upper secondary schools there are 16 national three year courses, differing in emphasis but mostly of at least 2 400 hours and all including the same eight core subjects. Two of the courses, those in the natural and social sciences, focus more on university entrance. Other national courses are more vocational and include a period, of about 10 weeks, of work experience. There are also some individual courses and some schools are independent. About a quarter of students leaving Swedish upper secondary schools continue their studies within three years at one or other of the country's 20 universities and colleges.

The distinction within three years, between FE and HE is made particularly clear in the **United Kingdom** by the fact that these two levels of education are overseen by two different funding councils. Further education can be offered in various types of establishment: for example, in schools run by local education authorities, in independent colleges, or in establishments run by business organisations or voluntary bodies. It can lead to national vocational qualifications that are either job-specific or more generally vocational, or it can lead to an extension of General Certificate in Secondary Education school leaving examination qualifications in conventional school subjects.

Higher education in the United Kingdom is undertaken mainly either in universities or in a variety of vocational, technical and art colleges. Vocational courses can prepare people for higher technician, management or professional jobs, and academic courses can lead to degree level and to postgraduate qualifications. Some establishments run both FE and HE courses.

B. THE POPULATION UNDER CONSIDERATION

In **Australia** the definition of disability used by the Australian Bureau of Statistics is based on that of the World Health Organisation. It is not, however, the only definition used in compiling Australian statistics concerning disability, and it is not always clear as to which definitions are being used in different regions. It is in essence the following:

Disability is the presence of one or more limitations, restrictions or impairments which has lasted, or is likely to last, for six months or more. A handicapped person is a disabled person aged five years or over who is further identified as being limited to some degree in the ability to perform certain tasks in relation to one of five areas: self-care; mobility; verbal communication; schooling; employment.

In 1993, 18 per cent of Australians were thought to be disabled, with 14.2 per cent both disabled and handicapped. These conditions were strongly related to age, the rates both for men and for women increasing rapidly beyond the age of 45. The main limitations among people with disabilities were in learning (28 per cent), mobility (21 per cent), hearing (12 per cent), vision (12 per cent), health (11 per cent) and manual dexterity (9 per cent).

A survey of students with disabilities receiving vocational education in **Finland** was conducted in 1995 by the National Board of Education. In the vocational institutions offering places to students generally, the main limitation of 29 per cent of those with disabilities was in academic learning. A further 27 per cent had been following a modified curriculum in their comprehensive schools, 19 per cent had emotional and behavioural difficulties, 9 per cent had a language disorder, 6 per cent had a developmental difficulty, 1.3 per cent had a physical disability, 1.5 per cent had hearing impairment and 0.6 per cent had visual impairment. In vocational institutions for students with disabilities, the most common limitations were physical (18 per cent), developmental (18 per cent), emotional (11 per cent), visual (7 per cent) and academic learning (7 per cent).

Among students with disabilities in higher education in **France** in 1995, the impairments of 36 per cent were motor, those of 19 per cent were visual and those of 15 per cent were auditory.

The percentage of people in the 15 to 26 year age range with disabilities in **Ireland** is not known. In further education, among those taking leaving certificate examinations in 1995, special arrangements were made for 317 students with auditory impairment, 141 were allowed visual aids and 152 had their question papers read to them. In 1993-94, at a rough estimate, some 400 students with disabilities were attending higher education institutions.

In **Italy**, the formal multi-disciplinary procedure for identifying disability results in a small proportion of children being certificated as having special educational needs and thus being entitled to extra educational help, provided in ordinary schools by specially trained support teachers. Ministry of Education statistics for the school year 1992/93 indicate that in that year 2 per cent of children of statutory school age had certificates. Certificates are reviewed annually and the system continues into further education, but in 1992/93 only 0.2 per cent of the upper secondary school population were recorded as having certificates. Within this 0.2 per cent, the main recorded disability of 78 per cent was psychophysical, for 15 per cent it was auditory and for 7 per cent it was visual.

In the **Netherlands**, the Inter-Ministerial Steering Group has considered in some detail the various definitions of impairment, disability and handicap, and their associated prevalence figures. The group reported in 1995 that findings from these different approaches converge to the extent that they can be fairly well represented by what is known as the concept of "triple trichotomy" (see Part I.B).

Within any one country, definitions may also vary according to context. The **Norwegian** report, for example, makes it clear that the term "disability" is being used there, within the context of education, with a meaning slightly different from that which is applied in a more general context. For instance, some people who meet the general criteria for disability, say through a physical impairment, can have their educational needs met without any particular adaptation to classrooms, teaching methods or teaching materials, so in the educational context they are not disabled. Official Norwegian reports draw on the following general definition of disability:

> A *person is disabled who, because of a chronic illness, injury or handicap, or because of social deviation, is severely restricted in the practical conduct of his or her life in relation to the surrounding community. This can apply to such matters as education, choice of vocation, occupation, or physical or cultural activities.*

In Norway, with disability defined within an educational context, among pupils reaching the age of completion of compulsory education, some 3 per cent are estimated to fall within this category, and virtually all of them take advantage of the priority accorded to them for places in upper secondary education. People having "severely impaired ability to work" are also considered to constitute 3 per cent of the population in the 16 to 25 age group, with this figure rising to 6 per cent in the 25 to 44 year age group.

Among the Norwegian students entering upper secondary school in 1989 with a recognised disability of educational significance, 68 per cent were male. The major categories of disability were illiteracy, innumeracy and mental retardation, together accounting for 57 per cent of those registered. Other disabilities included emotional difficulties, medical conditions, sensory impairment and motor disability. Among the occupationally disabled adults in Norway in 1991, 60 per cent were male. Of the total, those with impairment of muscles, joints or vertebrae accounted for 33 per cent and those with social/psychological problems a further 21 per cent.

A survey carried out in **Spain** by the National Statistics Institute in 1986 indicated that 15 per cent of adults had some form of disability. However, only 6 per cent of the adult population were thought to experience a significant level of handicap. The larger percentage included mild disabilities, defined in accordance with the World Health Organisation's 1980 International Classification of Impairments, Disabilities and Handicaps. Among those with handicaps in the 18 to 64 year age range, and with some having more than one handicap, 71 per cent had a physical disability, 21 per cent a learning difficulty and 23 per cent a sensory impairment, with limitations in vision predominating slightly over those in hearing.

In **Sweden**, very few individuals are officially designated as having disabilities. For example, only 1.5 per cent of Swedish pupils of school age are considered to have functional impairment. This consists of 0.09 per cent with visual impairment, 0.26 per cent with a physical handicap, 0.34 per cent with a hearing disability and 0.85 per cent with a learning difficulty.

The results of surveys undertaken in the **United Kingdom** by the Office of Population Censuses and Surveys between 1985 and 1988, using the World Health Organisation's classification, indicated that 14 per cent of the total adult population had at least one disability.

C. POLICIES AND LEGISLATION

Australia has a strong commitment to social justice and equity policies for people with disabilities. Policy in recent years, underpinned by principles of normalisation and least restrictive environment, has been firmly in favour of community support as opposed to segregated services. The under-representation of people with disabilities in tertiary education and training is recognised and a long-standing government objective is to increase their participation.

In Australia, the Disability Discrimination Act of 1992 makes it unlawful to discriminate against people on the grounds of their disabilities. It embodies the principle of making "reasonable adjustments", so that people with disabilities are not subject to "unjustifiable hardship". In education this includes adjusting physical access, curriculum design, teaching methods, and assessment procedures.

Adult special education was recognised as *a priori*ty in **British Columbia** in a 1982 Policy Statement, with its priority status confirmed in a review undertaken in 1990. A Ministry-funded report issued in 1993 on post-secondary education for people with disabilities, however, claimed that existing legislation did not protect these people's interests and recommended that the government pass equal access legislation, establishing an Equal Access Council to promote and monitor compliance with this legislation.

Under the national 1993-1996 Vocational Rehabilitation of Disabled Persons Act and Agreement between Human Resources Development Canada and each province's Ministry of Skills, Training and Labour (MSTL), in British Columbia the MSTL runs a range of Vocational Rehabilitation Services (VRS) programmes designed to help people with disabilities enter the labour market.

In 1978 the **Quebec** National Assembly passed the Exercise of Rights (Disabled Persons) Act, formally adopted a social integration policy for people with disabilities in 1985 and has put this policy into practice through subsequent legislation.

While collaboration among education, health, social services and other agencies is well recognised in **Finland** as being necessary for the interests of students with disabilities to be met, there is some dissatisfaction as to the extent to which this occurs. This was a finding resulting from an enquiry in 1995 from the National Board of Education to associations concerned with disabilities. The associations thought that there was insufficient legislation concerning inter-agency co-operation.

In segregated provision, students with disabilities in Finland have free accommodation, educational materials and health and welfare services. In integrated provision, they can be helped through an act concerning support for people with disabilities. This entitles them to transport services and any escorting needed to enable them to travel to their place of study, interpreter services, and if necessary a personal assistant.

Post-compulsory education in **France** is governed by the Framework Education Law of 10 July 1989, which lays down the principles that all students leaving compulsory education without a recognised level of attainment should be allowed to continue their studies in order to reach that level and that their knowledge and skills should be assessed to enable them to build career paths. The law also sets national targets to be achieved by the year 2000. The importance of vocational objectives is recognised in the Circular of 31 March 1992, which affirms that secure employment is just as valid an objective for the education system as examination success or further education.

Iceland recognises its commitment, for example through its membership of the United Nations, to providing education for all, including those with a disability. Further education, taking place mainly in upper secondary schools, is governed by legislation originating in 1988 and subjected to later amendments. This legislation stipulates that anyone who has completed compulsory education or who has reached the age of 18 years has the right to enter a course of studies at the upper secondary level. Provision is funded nationally, although local authorities meet 40 per cent of the construction costs of new buildings. While there is no Icelandic legislation covering higher education as a whole, there is legislation specific to each higher education institution, stating its main roles, organisation and educational programmes.

Government policy in **Ireland** is to have a continuum of provision, ranging flexibly from occasional help in ordinary schools to full-time enrolment in special schools. A general acceptance of the need for a substantial degree of integration of people with and without disabilities is reflected in the recently published Government White Paper on education, which confirms all students' right of access to and participation in the educational system, and in the 1993 report of the Special Education Review Committee. In the light of the recommendations of this committee and of recent court judgements, the Interdepartmental Co-ordinating Committee, with representation from the Departments of Education and Health, has been established to co-ordinate policies and monitor services

The 1992 law on adult education in Ireland states that adults can obtain education for pleasure or for the development of skills, and there is an education centre for adults with severe learning difficulties. The rights of students with disabilities are consolidated by the 1992 Act on the Affairs of the Handicapped, which has the objective "to ensure to the handicapped equality and living conditions comparable with those of other citizens, and to provide them with conditions that enable them to lead a normal life". While these laws are facilitating, Ireland does not have an up-to-date legal framework for education. Because of this, there are uncertainties as to the extent to which children with disabilities have rights of access to education. A Commission on the status of people with disabilities, established in 1993, is preparing guidelines which should eventually result in legal reform.

Since the mid-1970s, **Italian** government policy has been consistently in favour of inclusive education, and much legislation has been enacted to implement this. The overall responsibility for education is divided between two closely linked ministries, the Ministry for Public Education and the Ministry for Universities and Scientific Research. They collaborate with the Budget, Treasury and Finance Ministries on all questions related to funding, and with the Labour and Social Security Ministry on issues linking schools and work.

Following an Italian court judgement of 1987, existing regulations concerning pupils with learning difficulties and disabilities were extended to embrace post-compulsory education. Provision for these students was further enhanced by a law of February 1992, which requires upper secondary schools to adapt premises and equipment, allocate support teachers, train these support teachers, and make special arrangements for examinations. The universities are required to adapt premises, provide technical support (including, for example, sign language interpreters in classes), train specialist teachers, make special examination arrangements, and undertake research into various aspects of disability.

In line with a general **Netherlands** policy of decentralisation, implementation from 1994 of the Services for the Handicapped Act has involved delegation of responsibilities for the post-compulsory education of people with disabilities to the municipalities. Policy concerning people with disabilities is formulated and co-ordinated by the Inter-ministerial Steering Group, which meets monthly and has outlined a programme of action for which seven members of the Cabinet have joint responsibilities. In 1995 the group stated basic principles underlying this policy to be threefold:

- equal rights, equal obligations, equal treatment;
- integration and participation; and
- wherever necessary, protection and compensation.

The extent to which policy concerning disability is implemented in the Netherlands is actively monitored by three research organisations: the Database of Research in the Field of Rehabilitation, the Handicapped and the Chronically Ill; the Knowledge Platform (a consortium of three research institutes); the Social and Cultural Planning Bureau.

From 1996, an act on vocational education in the Netherlands has provided for co-ordination of facilities for further education through the development of regional education centres, which will eventually offer the full range of further educational provision, for adults as well as for school leavers, including special educational facilities such as adult basic education in literacy and numeracy. The Disabled Workers Employment Act gives formal approval to the country's five revalidation centres run specifically for people with disabilities and establishes a quota system whereby 3 per cent to 7 per cent of each employer's workforce must be people with disabilities.

In **Norway**, for over 25 years the principle of normalisation has pervaded consideration of people with disabilities. In 1968, the government endorsed the view that society must as far as possible adapt to the needs of disabled people rather than expect them one-sidedly to adapt themselves to society. Subsequent measures for those with disabilities have been incorporated within those applying to people more generally.

All young people in Norway have a statutory right to three years of further education after completion of schooling at the age of 16. The Upper Secondary School Act of 1974 states that those requiring special educational help shall receive it. Applicants with disabilities, subject to their having been assessed as requiring education adapted to meet their special needs, are entitled to be admitted to the foundation course of their choice in the first year of upper secondary school and may continue to receive further education for up to five years, or until they reach the age of 22. The National Insurance Act ensures that they have the necessary financial support.

Spain follows international guidelines with respect to the education and employment of people with disabilities. The Spanish government has an interdepartmental body, presided over by the Queen, to promote and co-ordinate social policies and practice with respect to people with disabilities. The 1982 Law of Social Integration of the Handicapped obliges enterprises with more than

50 workers to have people with disabilities constituting up to 2 per cent of its workforce; in public administration the figure is 3 per cent.

In **Swedish** society the principles of equality and normalisation have been well established for many years, with the emphasis on acknowledging people's strengths and potential rather than dwelling on their disabilities. However, while much progress has been made towards translating these principles into practice, it is recognised that people with disabilities continue to be disadvantaged.

In the **United Kingdom**, government policy states that learning difficulty or disability should not be a bar on access to further or higher education, and recognises the necessity of inter-agency collaboration in identifying people with disabilities and in meeting their needs. Representatives from some 15 government departments meet regularly to co-ordinate the country's disability policy.

In the United Kingdom, the 1992 Further and Higher Education Act secures access to full-time suitable further education for all young people over compulsory school age and under 19 years of age. For students with special educational needs, the specified range of offerings includes courses in independent living, in communication skills, in basic literacy and in basic numeracy. Through Training and Enterprise Councils (TECs), young people and adults of working age who are neither in full-time education nor in employment have access to vocational training programmes, and those with disabilities have priority status, with extra funding allowed where necessary, for example for residential training.

The 1986 Disabled Persons Act, as amended by the 1992 Further and Higher Education Act, requires education, health, social services and further education agencies in the United Kingdom to collaborate in exchanging information conducive to meeting the needs of students with disabilities. Where establishments for post-compulsory education do not have suitable facilities for young people with learning difficulties or disabilities, the Further Education Funding Council has the duty to fund provision for them, up to the age of 25 years, at independent specialist establishments. Again, where it is warranted, funding may cover the cost of boarding accommodation as well as that of tuition.

There is no legislation in the United Kingdom governing higher education provision for students with disabilities, and the institutions are left to determine their own provision for such people. There is, however, a Disability Discrimination Bill which, if it becomes law, will require institutions for further and higher education to publicise their facilities for students with disabilities.

D. TRANSITION FROM SCHOOLING

Although transition planning is not mandatory in **Australia**, initiatives have been set up in schools to prepare pupils with disabilities reaching the end of the age range of statutory schooling for their next steps, and survey data indicate that, in 1993, 46 per cent of these 15-year-olds, ranging from 26 per cent in ordinary classes to 55 per cent in special schools and 59 per cent in special classes, had individual plans. They form part of a whole life plan which includes the provision of relevant curricula during the upper secondary years, provision of information to help decision-making regarding post-school options, and liaison with adult training agencies. Individual transition planning teams involve the student, the family, the school and other relevant agencies in individual goal-setting activities.

Reports from transition experts in Australia indicate that students with disabilities require longer time in transition into and through the levels of post-compulsory education. This is confirmed by the government report of 1993 that students with disabilities in higher education tend to be older than those without disabilities.

In comprehensive schools in **Finland**, all students are entitled to counselling and to vocational guidance, and there is generally a person in the school with training in and responsibility for these services. In special education, these responsibilities are generally undertaken by the class teachers. To help students with disabilities, a psychologist may be consulted and vocational tests may be used, but in most areas of the country such services are not called upon as much as they could be. Up to 15 days may be used for familiarisation visits to possible places of work or further education, and studies of the transition of students with disabilities have recommended an extension of these arrangements.

Under the Comprehensive School Act, staff of secondary schools in Finland have the duty to continue to support their students with special needs after they have moved on to employment or further study. They are required to pass information concerning the students' characteristics on to further education establishments. In practice, however, sometimes to preserve confidentiality or to avoid giving a student a bad name, comprehensive schools do not always meet these requirements. Transition arrangements for students in special schools are generally managed more effectively.

Establishments offering vocational training in Finland usually employ social workers who liaise with the schools. Sometimes school and vocational institute have the same social worker, and this is beneficial. Liaison managed by the vocational institutions for students with disabilities is usually better staffed and more effective than that managed by the general vocational institutions, as are preliminary visits, preparation studies, selection courses and trial placements.

In **Iceland**, no special arrangements exist in schools. Work centres run by local authorities have a duty to provide occupational counselling for school leavers with disabilities and find suitable employment for them.

Transition to post-compulsory education in **Ireland** is helped by the fact that the junior secondary cycle, occurring over the three years to the end of compulsory schooling at 15, and the senior secondary cycle, which can last for the three years following this, take place in the same school. Assessment is both continuous, through teacher observation, and summative, through examinations, and schools have people with responsibilities for careers guidance. For students taking public examinations at the end of the junior or senior secondary cycle, special arrangements can be made to compensate for any sensory, motor or specific literacy difficulties.

The Rehabilitation Institute, an Irish voluntary body, runs a one-year college course, leading to the Higher Leaving Certificate, specially designed to prepare students with disabilities for entry to higher education. While higher education institutions are increasingly aware of the needs of students with disabilities and while many have a disability officer who co-ordinates their support, the Association for Higher Education Access and Disability (AHEAD) found recently that some 22 per cent still restrict their entry, often on the grounds that on scientific and technical courses they would not be able to do the practical work.

While there is open entrance to **Italian** upper secondary schools, guidance concerning suitable pathways is provided in schools towards the end of lower secondary schooling. For pupils with certificates of special educational need, the system whereby certificates are reviewed annually provides an opportunity for post-compulsory education and training needs to be considered on an inter-disciplinary basis.

In **Norway**, staff of the local authorities' educational psychological services assess school leavers and provide upper secondary school admission boards with expert opinions as to which of their applicants are entitled to the priority accorded to students with disabilities. They also make sure that contact with the further establishment is made well before the pupil leaves school, co-ordinate relevant information on the pupil's disabilities for the benefit of the further education establishment and comment on any curriculum modification that may be required following transition.

In **Spain**, the 1990 Law of General Regulation of the Educational System requires that each pupil reaching the end of compulsory education will have a "guidance counsel", which will summarise the extent to which the pupil has achieved set educational objectives, will refer to social development and will comment on prospects for future academic education, vocational training or employment. While in practice schools still vary in the extent to which they have developed the resources to meet this requirement, it should eventually facilitate transition. It is planned that form teachers and educational psychologists will collaborate in providing the reports.

Each school in **Sweden** has a member of staff who provides guidance to all pupils both on further education options and on opportunities for employment.

In their work with pupils with disabilities these members of staff are advised by people with expertise in careers aspects of disability who are employed by the municipalities and who receive extra remuneration from the Swedish Agency for Special Education.

In the **United Kingdom**, where in January 1994 just under one child in 40 of school age had a formal statement of special educational need, local education authorities are required under the 1993 Education Act to formally review these statements as children approach school leaving age. Regulations introduced in 1994 require local education authorities to invite parents, social workers and careers officers to the review meetings. The review culminates in the formulation of a transition plan, designed to ensure that relevant information possessed by the education, employment, health and welfare agencies is drawn together to produce an action plan that will as far as possible enable the young person to meet his or her educational, leisure and vocational needs on reaching school leaving age.

E.   FUNDING

Since 1983, expenditure on education in **Australia** has increased in real terms by 46 per cent, to over A$10 billion in 1994-95, with particularly marked increases in support for vocational programmes. Most of the funding to support people with disabilities is provided to the educational institutions through grants or block funding. Additional funds are provided by the government's Department of Employment, Education and Training to targeted individual students. Eligibility for disability support pensions and associated allowances is assessed through local disability panels. Extra cost per annum per student was calculated in one region to be A$2 500 for visual disability, A$1 800 for auditory, A$1 200 for physical and A$700 for intellectual.

Between 1985 and 1991 the budget for support services for students with disabilities in post-compulsory education in **British Columbia** increased more than sixfold. The Ministry provides targeted funding to further and higher education establishments for support services for students with disabilities. In addition, two establishments have funding to operate province-wide services: in one, a library for students with visual impairment; in the other, an interpretation service for those with hearing impairment. The University of British Columbia receives provincial government funding for its Disability Resource Centre. The costs of the province's Vocational Rehabilitation Services (VRS) are shared between federal and provincial budgets.

The two general and vocational colleges serving as centres of excellence for the education of students with disabilities in **Quebec** receive a budget allocated from the government and use it for the benefit of the students with disabilities attending all of the 49 colleges designated as providing for them. For example, the two centres may provide sound recordings, Braille texts or personal escorts for students in the other colleges. Individual students, whether or not they have disabilities, may be able to get grants or obtain student loans. There is also an allowances scheme for special needs, through which students with disabilities may be paid costs, for example, of transport or of transliteration of texts.

Since the beginning of 1993, **Finland** has had a state grant system, designed to delegate to the municipalities and in some cases directly to the local educational establishments most of the decision-making concerning the allocation of funds to the various aspects of education. Grants to vocational institutions are allocated in accordance with student numbers and the average cost per unit for the type of institution. Each student with a disability in an ordinary institution, however, counts as 1.5, which is the unit cost per student in a special education institution. Within special education institutions, students with severe disabilities count as 1.5 times the unit cost in those institutions.

Individual students in full-time post-compulsory education in Finland, if in need of financial aid, may be able to obtain non-repayable grants, housing benefits and study loans. Students with disabilities may also be eligible for a nationally distributed rehabilitation allowance or disability pension, and through municipal funding they may be able to obtain finance for transport, an interpreter and/or a personal assistant. In recent years, limitations in allocation of funding to education generally have adversely affected the adaptation of accommodation, the teaching arrangements for students with disabilities and the support services available to them.

In **Iceland**, the government funds the teaching provided in further education and in higher education. At both levels, students with disabilities are eligible for the financial assistance available to students generally. If they do not qualify for this, they may be able to get financial support under the Act on the Affairs of the Handicapped.

Funding for students with disabilities in **Ireland** is mainly from public taxation and from the European Social Fund, with some additional support through voluntary organisations and religious orders. The Department of Education pays for school buildings, staff salaries and student transport, and the Ministry of Health's local health boards manage support services external to schools. The National Rehabilitation Board co-ordinates and monitors vocational training programmes for people with disabilities. Some of these programmes qualify for support from the European Social Fund. There is a limited number of additional university grants for which students with disabilities can apply.

The funding of upper secondary schools in **Italy** is managed by the Ministry for Public Education and that of universities by the Ministry for Universities and

Scientific Research. On all questions relating to funding both ministries collaborate with the Budget, Treasury and Finance Ministries. The Ministry for Public Education transfers most of the upper secondary school funding for staff, school buildings, transport and teaching materials to provincial offices or to individual schools. Any attempts to calculate the cost of providing education for students with special needs are complicated by the fact that a significant part of the cost, notably that of some of the external support services, is borne by the health authorities.

In **Norway**, further education in the upper secondary schools is funded through lump sum transfer from the government to the regional authorities and in the 1988/89 academic year special education measures accounted for 7.5 per cent of the total operating budget. Special education courses for adults, under the Adult Education Act, may have their costs met by the government. Enterprises taking on apprentices receive locally administered grants, and those taking on apprentices with disabilities can receive up to three times the normal allowance, if the training can be demonstrated to involve extra costs.

The National Insurance Act in Norway provides for financial support for the rehabilitation of people who "because of sickness, injury or handicap" have a permanently reduced ability to do paid work or have a substantially restricted choice of occupation or workplace. Under this act, students with disabilities on further education or higher education courses may be supported to meet the costs of personal help, transport or special equipment.

In **Spain**, as far as the education of students with disabilities generally is concerned, there are no budgets beyond those available to all students. There are, however, mechanisms whereby some students may be able to obtain special equipment, teaching programmes or, in the case of students with hearing impairment, the help of people able to mediate between speech and sign language.

Responsibilities for public services in **Sweden** for students with disabilities mostly follow those for people generally. The state has overall responsibility for social insurance, for the educational framework and for the planning of welfare. Health services are delegated to regional level, and municipalities carry responsibilities for education up to university level, for housing and for child care. Contrary to the general pattern, special schools and some special education programmes are run not by the municipalities but by the state. Within each municipality, social services are run by agencies. Some people with disabilities are entitled to home services, the fees for which are based on income, and which may include a personal assistant.

In the **United Kingdom**, funding is supplied directly from the government's Further Education Funding Council to the further education establishments and takes into account the needs of students with learning difficulties and disabilities.

With respect to each student it consists of three elements: an entry element, designed to encourage colleges to assess individual needs; a programme element, providing extra money for students needing extra support; and an achievement element, linked to the achievement of set learning goals.

Money is also allocated to colleges in the United Kingdom for capital projects and for equipment, and this includes a proportion reflecting individuals' needs for extra support, but the colleges are free to make their own decisions as to how much of it they spend for the benefit of students with disabilities. Entry to further education is free for full-time students aged 16+ to 18+. The colleges can set their own fees for older students, but for those receiving disability benefits they may waive the fees and be compensated by the funding council for doing so.

Vocational training for unemployed people is paid for by the government through allocations to Training and Enterprise Councils, which in turn pay commercial organisations running "Training for Work" programmes. Payments are weighted in favour of unemployed people with disabilities. In all these programmes the expected outcomes are stated at the beginning and 25 per cent of the payment is conditional on achievement of these stated outcomes. The country's Youth Training Scheme for school leavers is funded similarly, except that here only 25 per cent of the payment is conditional on outcomes.

In the United Kingdom, the funding council concerned with higher education has for the past two years granted money to help institutions improve physical access for students with disabilities, and 86 projects have been supported in this way. Higher education students with disabilities are able to obtain allowances, additional to their means-tested mandatory awards, to help them meet the costs of any personal help, transport or equipment they may need.

F.   PROVISION

Between 1982 and 1992 the proportion of **Australians** continuing in education beyond the compulsory age range doubled, to over 70 per cent. Pupils with disabilities, however, are twice as likely to leave school before reaching final year standards as are other pupils and many of them do not undertake any post-compulsory education or training. Among students in education at senior secondary level, 4 per cent are considered to be disabled. With 18 per cent of the adult population identified as disabled and with prevalence being higher among older people, this suggests that only about a quarter of those with disabilities reaching the end of the compulsory school age range remain in education.

The technical and further education colleges of Australia have developed a framework for enhancing their provision for students with disabilities through a 1994-96 initiative, "FlexA*bility*", which aims to raise the participation rate of students with disabilities from less than 1 per cent of their total enrolment in 1992 to 10 per cent in 2001.

The participation rate for people with disabilities in the Australian labour force in 1993 was 46 per cent and that for those without disabilities was 77 per cent. As means of overcoming disadvantages experienced by people with disabilities trying to gain employment, various programmes have been developed. Some offer specialised assessment and tailored placement, some provide social or vocational training, some meet the extra costs to employees of getting to work, some subsidise employers.

While entry to Australian universities is competitive and based on academic merit, various equity provisions are made for those with disabilities. In addition, for any students, there is access to higher education courses on a distance learning basis without any pre-requisite academic achievements. These courses are run by a consortium of universities, the government-funded Open Learning Agency of Australia, and can be of particular use to some students with disabilities.

In the Canadian province of **British Columbia**, during the 1980s, most institutions developed their own adult special education policies and opportunities increased significantly, with full-time places in adult special education programmes increasing from 384 to 689 between 1985 and 1991. Nevertheless, a review in 1990 found that accessibility was still limited. Despite further improvement, this continues to be the case and advocacy groups have sought a strengthening of rights through legislation.

Specific measures to secure inclusive further education for students with disabilities in **Quebec** began in the 1980s, when two colleges were specially designated to receive students with disabilities. The colleges became centres of excellence, helped other institutions develop similar skills and by 1995 a total of 49 general and vocational colleges were operating in this way, each supported by a range of education, health and welfare services. Numbers of students with disabilities benefiting from college provision have risen progressively, from 21 in 1983 to 406 in 1994. Most students with disabilities attend ordinary classes and colleges can only refuse admission to these classes if they can demonstrate beyond all doubt that they are unable to make the adaptations necessary.

Whereas about half the lower secondary school leavers in **Finland** go on to further education in senior secondary schools, only a third of those with visual disabilities, 88 per cent of whom have been educated in ordinary schools, do so. Almost a third of those with visual disabilities stay on at school for an extra year after reaching the end of their period of compulsory schooling, whereas in the age group as a whole only 8 per cent stay on. Over the 1981-93 period, an average of 70 per cent of comprehensive school leavers with emotional and behavioural difficulties went on to further education but 46 per cent of those who were admitted dropped out.

Further education is available to all students reaching the end of their compulsory schooling in Finland. In 1988 there were 193 students with disabilities in senior secondary schools, 298 in folk high schools and 3 371 in vocational training. Of those in vocational training, 64 per cent were in vocational institutions, 19 per cent in commercial colleges and 10 per cent in adult education centres.

By 1995, approximately 2 per cent of the total number of students in vocational training establishments for students generally in Finland were students with disabilities. Among 3 916 students with disabilities, 78 per cent were in vocational institutions and most of the remainder were in establishments concerned with particular fields of study, including home economics, commerce, agriculture, craft and design, and technology. Some 400 students with disabilities are in the country's 90 folk high schools, all of which are run on a residential basis, and in the main they follow social training programmes, with 162 of them in the three folk high schools providing specifically for students with disabilities.

In 1995, there were a further 2 987 students enrolled, mostly on a full-time basis, in one or other of Finland's 15 vocational training institutions providing specifically for students with disabilities, with students' average ages running from about 20 to over 30. Nine of these institutions are independent, run by associations concerned with particular disabilities but given state support. Among these students, the institutions themselves named 42 per cent as having severe disability, each thus attracting 50 per cent extra funding. These institutions can fill up empty places with students who do not have disabilities and in three of the institutions such students constituted more than 20 per cent of the total on roll.

Applications for entry to further education establishments in Finland are dealt with through a joint selection system in the case of ordinary vocational institutions, by the individual institution in the case of the folk high schools, and by both methods in the case of the vocational institutions providing specially for students with disabilities.

In 1994, 1 158 students with disabilities applied through Finland's joint selection system, 878 of them having just left comprehensive school or special school, and 73 per cent succeeded, including almost all those seeking special class places in ordinary vocational institutions. Reasons for rejection included poor health, low ability, emotional and behavioural difficulties and, in the case of some with sensory or motor impairment, limitations of staffing or premises.

Only about half the applicants to special vocational institutions in Finland are admitted. Reasons for rejection include students' already having received vocational education, poor health, absence of suitable courses, too slight a disability and poor motivation.

Among people with disabilities in **France** continuing their education beyond the school leaving age of 16, as a result of integration policies, over the past five years the number achieving the B*accalauréat* and then going on to higher education has increased by almost 20 per cent annually, reaching 4 000 in 1995. This continues to be a minority, however.

The majority of school leavers with disabilities in France, some 40 000 in 1994, who will usually have spent much of their compulsory schooling in special classes or special schools, attend courses known as "special general and vocational courses". These courses can enable them to achieve a certificate of professional competence (the ordinary school leaving *Certificat d'Aptitude Professionnelle*, or CAP). Unqualified school leavers who move directly into employment may gain their certificates through part-time attendance at apprenticeship training centres.

People with severe disabilities in France, who are likely to have been schooled in special educational/medical institutes, tend to remain in this kind of special setting, moving from the age of 14 into vocational/medical institutes and taking pre-vocational or vocational courses. Courses can last for up to eight years and about half those completing them gain regular employment within two years, with numbers entering open employment and numbers entering sheltered employment being approximately equal.

In **Iceland**, while not all school leavers with disabilities are offered the further education placements of their choice, practically all get an offer of some kind, in upper secondary schools, in special centres or in both. The special habilitation centres, the rehabilitation centres, the day care centres and the sheltered workshops provide social training and vocational training.

Among people with disabilities beyond the age of compulsory schooling in **Ireland**, the percentage receiving education or training in integrated settings is not known. Among the country's second-level schools, which enrol young people for the three years up to the end of statutory schooling and for the three years beyond it, five have been designated to make special provision for students with disabilities but, in accordance with the wishes of parents, ordinary neighbourhood schools are increasingly taking on students with disabilities. Most of the country's 115 special schools have places for students in the 15 to 18 year age range.

Entry to the senior cycle of secondary education in Ireland is open to all students in the 15 to 18 year age range. Guidance concerning subsequent education and training may be offered by staff of the school, by psychologists and others employed by local health agencies, or through assessment conducted by the vocational guidance officers of the National Rehabilitation Board. While entry to higher education is dependent on success in the Leaving Certificate examinations, usually taken at the age of 18, some universities and colleges grant special interviews to students with disabilities who may have under-performed in examinations.

Entrance to the upper secondary schools in **Italy** is entirely a matter for parental and student choice, though academic and vocational guidance is provided for pupils approaching the end of their statutory schooling.

In the **Netherlands**, with some 4 per cent of all children of compulsory school age attending special schools, students can continue there up to the age of 20 years, and beyond this in exceptional cases. Individuals' special school placements are re-examined by a board of experts every two years, to determine whether the placements should continue.

Among people with disabilities aged 18 to 45 in the Netherlands, the proportion having achieved a secondary or higher level of education is only about half that in the age range as a whole, and among those leaving special schools 28 per cent do not continue into post-compulsory education. The Centre for Vocational Orientation and Training reported in 1992 that only 15 per cent of the people with disabilities eligible for vocational education were enrolled.

In **Norway**, the large majority of students with disabilities in the 16 to 18 year age range receive further education in the upper secondary schools, in either ordinary or special classes, with the emphasis of the latter being on social skills. A survey in 1989, however, indicated that only some 20 per cent of them completed the full three years. The 1994 change in regulations, ensuring that people with disabilities can be given up to five years in further education, may change this position considerably. In 1992/93, some 8 per cent of students with disabilities were educated outside the ordinary upper secondary school system, in either special upper secondary schools or in other special institutions, for example in residential centres for those with hearing or visual impairment.

Education at basic school level is also provided in Norway for adults with learning difficulties, some of these difficulties having been present throughout life and some having arisen in adulthood through accident or illness. In 1992, 2 824 men and 2 422 women over 21 received education of this kind, and numbers in subsequent years have been similar. A broader range of leisure, vocational and academic courses is organised through the co-operation of Norway's 26 organisations for people with disabilities. In 1994 there were 2 800 such initiatives nationally, with 22 500 participants attending for a total of 103 000 hours.

The proportion of higher education students with disabilities in Norway is not known. In one university, however, which has good physical access facilities for students with disabilities and which therefore is almost certainly atypical, some 2 per cent of entrants asked for adapted study or examination conditions.

Students with disabilities can be admitted to Norwegian universities and colleges of higher education without their having to meet conventional entrance requirements. Virtually all the 3 per cent of school leavers assessed as having educational disabilities receive further education in upper secondary school, with most of them opting for vocational training.

In **Spain**, the percentage of school leavers with disabilities participating in further education is not known, but it is believed to be the majority. Most are enrolled on programmes which offer vocational training but do not necessarily lead to qualifications. Social training programmes exist, but they are scattered geographically, often run privately, and generally not well resourced. Few students with disabilities enter higher education, though some of the universities are taking steps to improve physical access and provide suitable programmes.

While most **Swedish** students with special needs in their early years of post-compulsory education attend ordinary classes in ordinary upper secondary schools, there are some exceptions, whereby the students remain in the upper secondary schools but follow special programmes in special classes, including some using sign language and thus providing an option for students with severe hearing impairment, and some specially designed for students with severe motor disability. Some of these special courses are run nationally, focus on vocational preparation, require four years and have a minimum teaching time of 3 600 hours.

In Sweden there are 3 777 students – 1.2 per cent of the total upper secondary school population – who attend special upper secondary schools for students with severe learning difficulties. At adult level there are 3 146 students – 2.2 per cent of the total adult school population – attending special adult schools for those with severe learning difficulties.

In the **United Kingdom**, among those beyond compulsory school age, the proportion of people with disabilities who are receiving some form of education or training is not known. In 1993-94, 56 079 students in further education were classed as having some form of learning difficulty or disability. The Further Education Funding Council has commissioned research to estimate numbers, participation rates, factors influencing participation and unmet educational needs. Among the 70 898 students admitted to higher education in 1994, 17 per cent declared themselves to have some form of learning difficulty or disability.

Whereas places on Youth Training Schemes in the United Kingdom are guaranteed to all 16- and 17-year-olds needing and wanting them, the guarantee is extended to 18 years for trainees whose start has been delayed through disability. People with disabilities do not have to satisfy the general requirement of having been unemployed for six months before starting on a Training for Work scheme. The percentage eligible for post-compulsory education but not receiving it is not known.

In the United Kingdom, the continuing funding of further education in individual institutions is conditional upon the institutions' assessment of students' progress and on the students' achievement of agreed objectives. Inspection by Further Education Funding Council staff indicates that most of the institutions have introduced screening procedures to identify those students needing help in developing the literacy and numeracy skills required for success on the courses for which they have enrolled. In the vocational training schemes, the Training and Enterprise Council ensures that entrants are assessed and that assessment is linked to individual training plans.

In higher education the pattern across the United Kingdom is much more variable. A few institutions run services which have effective mechanisms for assessment and support, and the presence of these services tends to result in a marked increase in the number of students declaring their need for help, particularly for help in developing literacy skills.

G. THE CURRICULUM

The aim in **Australia** is for students with disabilities to have full access to an inclusive curriculum where possible but if necessary to make use of curriculum modification or special programmes of study. Most university policies, for example, state that, while maintaining standards and essential content, they will adapt teaching methods and course requirements to meet the needs of individuals.

Modifications to buildings in Australia include adaptations to enhance physical access (*e.g.* through ramps and handrails), sensory access (*e.g.* through tactile signs and audio cues) and communication access (*e.g.* through pictorial signs). Modifications to courses include selecting relevant modules, revising goals, adjusting duration, facilitating home study, changing teaching strategies, altering assessment methods, and providing technological support.

The 1990 review of the implementation of **British Columbia**'s policy according priority to adult special education involved surveys, meetings among stakeholders and input from an advisory committee which included community representation. It led to government initiatives resulting in improvements in accessibility of institutions, in integrated programmes, in support services and in co-ordination across institutions.

Students with disabilities in **Quebec** follow the full range of college courses. They are more likely to follow courses in the social sciences and in administration, and less likely to follow courses in the natural sciences, than are other students.

In Quebec, since 1976, the Building Code has ensured that new public buildings provide physical access for people with disabilities, although some of the older buildings are still in the process of being adapted. In over 30 of the general and vocational colleges, oral and sign interpreting services are provided for students with hearing impairment.

In **Finnish** institutions training students in catering, media, seafaring, social services, technology and health care, provision is adjusted to enable students with disabilities to obtain the same qualifications as the other students. In institutions providing training in economics, craft, design, agriculture and forestry, there may be some variations for students with disabilities in qualifications obtained as well as in admission requirements, duration of courses and methods of assessment.

Vocational education in Finland occurs within a national curriculum framework introduced in 1995. In ordinary vocational institutions, the courses most commonly followed by students with disabilities continue to be in home economics, cooking, cleaning, metalwork, vehicle maintenance and building construction. The range of subjects followed in the 15 special vocational institutions is similar, and vocational training is accompanied by counselling, independence training and some basic academic education.

In Finland's folk high schools the emphasis of special education is on independence training and on basic courses preparing students for vocational training. There are also evening schools which arrange short courses to meet the local needs of people with disabilities on, for example, sports, reading, cooking, achieving independence and personal relationships.

New buildings in Finland are designed to meet the needs of students with physical disabilities. The introduction of the new national curriculum framework into vocational education in 1995 has opened up possibilities for providing individually modified curricula for students with disabilities, for example by allowing more time to complete the same amount of work. National organisations concerned with severe learning disabilities and with visual impairment produce adapted education materials, most of which are at school level but some are designed for adults and are of use in vocational training.

The results of an enquiry conducted by the National Board of Education in Finland in 1995 indicated that among students with disabilities enrolled at vocational institutions in Finland, the proportion dropping out was high. Reasons given included large teaching groups, the time needed by the students, their adverse effects on other students, safety factors, staff attitudes, lack of knowledge and expertise among staff, lack of appropriate equipment, and lack of time to plan individual education programmes. The fact that teachers' salaries are tied to the number of hours they teach is a further impediment, as this discourages planning.

A study published in 1993 indicated that only a quarter of teachers in ordinary vocational institutions in Finland thought that students with disabilities should be educated inclusively. Half thought they should be in special classes and 15 per cent thought they should be in special institutions.

While new buildings in Finland are designed to meet the needs of students with physical disabilities, very little adaptation has been made to existing buildings. Whereas team teaching was used formerly for classes including students with disabilities, following funding restrictions the facility of having a second teacher has now been withdrawn. While the introduction of the new national curriculum framework into vocational education in 1995 has opened up possibilities for providing individually modified curricula for students with disabilities, these have not been put into practice as yet.

The 50 per cent extra funds allocated for students with disabilities in ordinary vocational training institutions in Finland have not been put to good use as yet, for example in planning individual education programmes, partly because of lack of expertise among teachers. While there are teaching materials designed for students with disabilities in schools, there is still a shortage of suitable materials in vocational training. Most of the training institutions rely on materials hand-made by the teachers. The availability of texts modified to meet the needs of students with visual impairment is limited, partly because of the expense of its production.

The National Board of Education undertakes annual follow-up of the use of funds allocated for special education in Finland and is successful in identifying inappropriate usage. The board's 1995 enquiry concerning vocational training for students with disabilities achieved only a 52 per cent response rate from the ordinary institutions. Nevertheless, this produced information valuable in planning further developments, and in addition representatives of the board visited all the vocational institutions providing specifically for students with disabilities. In 1995 the board also arranged training in institutions' self-assessment, and the vocational institutions for students with disabilities are now all involved in quality development projects.

Further education in **Iceland**'s upper secondary schools takes place within the framework of national curriculum guidelines. For example, academic courses leading to the standard leaving qualification have to include certain subjects, together comprising between 50 per cent and 80 per cent of the course: modern foreign languages, Icelandic, science, mathematics, social studies, physical education, computer studies. The schools' academic and vocational courses are open to students with disabilities and are generally followed by them.

In Iceland, while most further education students with disabilities follow the ordinary curriculum, they are helped as necessary through extra support teachers, for example through sign language interpreters, or through technical aids, for example through computers. Some have extra help to enable them to overcome literacy problems. Some follow a modified curriculum in special classes.

The students found the most difficult to provide for in Iceland are those with behavioural difficulties. Some of the upper secondary schools are not able to meet fully the needs of students with literacy problems.

While students with disabilities in the 15 to 18 year age range in **Ireland** are in principle free to follow any of the senior secondary cycle programmes, in practice some with sensory or motor disabilities are precluded from practical subjects, sometimes through over-caution on the part of themselves, their teachers or their parents rather than because of real hazard.

Regulations in Ireland state that all new school and college buildings must be completely accessible to students with disabilities and many of the older buildings have been adapted to the extent that they too now meet this criterion. Many students with disabilities in the 15 to 18 year age range take one subject less than their peers. This may be to allow for lack of stamina, to allow extra time to the subjects taken, or to create opportunities to acquire skills of particular value to them, for example in using computers.

Some students of post-compulsory age attend one or other of the Irish secondary schools' 48 special classes, where they follow a modified curriculum including communication skills, numeracy, social development and health education. If they reach the required standards they may then attend community workshops, designed to help a small number of people with disabilities to enter either open or sheltered employment.

In the **Italian** model, one aim is to ensure continuity of education for students of all abilities. In furtherance of this aim, those with disabilities follow the normal curriculum as far as possible, in ordinary classrooms. Those with certificates of special educational need are provided with extra individual help, through the allocation of support teachers with special training, to enable them to do this. When this is not possible, they usually remain in ordinary classes but follow individual education programmes specially designed to meet their needs.

Among the 35 respondents to a questionnaire distributed to the 60 Italian universities in 1994, statements indicated that 34 had plans to make premises accessible to students with disabilities, 31 had lifts, 30 had ramps, 16 provided technical support, 9 had toilet facilities and 7 had specially equipped classrooms.

Studies in the **Netherlands** reported by the Social and Cultural Planning Bureau in 1996 showed the participation rate in adult education among people with disabilities to be much lower than would be expected on the basis of demographic data. Findings also showed that institutions for adult education lacked the policies, buildings, equipment, knowledge and skills needed to facilitate access for people with disabilities to suitable courses.

Among people with disabilities entering vocational education in the Netherlands, a report by the Centre for Vocational Education and Training in 1992 indicated that 250 of the total of 1 250 attended one or other of the country's five special education centres, with the rest fairly equally distributed across the apprenticeship system, senior secondary vocational education, and adult vocational training centres. The report advocated that much more emphasis be placed on the senior secondary education and on the apprenticeship opportunities rather than on segregated provision. It did comment, however, that while these five national centres tended to operate in "splendid isolation" their quality of education and their output to the labour market were satisfactory.

In **Norway**, 45 per cent of students with disabilities taking further education courses in the upper secondary schools in 1992/93 followed individually designed curricula, for example by drawing on different elements of existing courses. Overall, some 70 per cent of students with disabilities in upper secondary schools take vocational courses, 20 per cent take courses combining vocational and social elements, and 7 per cent take academic courses.

When students in Norway are preparing for skilled trades, in accordance with the 1993 Act relating to vocational training, two years at the upper secondary school are followed by specialisation at a training establishment. Vocational training for young people with disabilities includes apprenticeship contracts that are adapted to take account of special needs. The Adult Education Act entitles adults with disabilities to receive education in the basic school curriculum if they need it, and people with visual or hearing impairment requiring rehabilitation courses can attend courses run by the relevant voluntary bodies and financed through the National Insurance Act.

Norwegian students in higher education take the regular courses with such adjustments to teaching and examinations as are needed. There is a general teacher training course specially designed for people with hearing impairment, with 38 places on offer.

In Norway, national building regulations specify that all public buildings, including further and higher education establishments, must be adapted to meet the needs for physical access of people with disabilities. Older schools are given extra allocations for building alterations. Each county has a technical aid centre which can help educational institutions adapt classrooms to meet the needs of students with sensory or motor impairment.

Students with disabilities following further education programmes in Norwegian upper secondary schools may attend regular classes with adaptation in certain subjects, for example by taking an introductory foundation class or by following a one-year course over two years, or they may attend special classes. Among students with disabilities entering upper secondary schools in 1992-93, 37 per cent attended special classes. In ordinary classes they may be given the support of an extra teacher.

When taking examinations, Norwegian students with disabilities may be given more time, may use special aids such as word processors, and in some cases may be given secretarial or interpreter services. Adapted teaching materials, such as tape recordings and Braille texts, may be obtainable from national or regional resource centres.

Among the 1992-93 national entry of students with disabilities to Norwegian upper secondary schools, 45 per cent followed individually designed curricula in some or all subjects. Among those with disabilities entering further education as a whole, 8 per cent were given special teaching at separate schools.

Higher education establishments in Norway do not offer alternative syllabi for students with disabilities, but they provide extra tutorial help. Two universities provide special services for students with disabilities and in 1994, some 2 per cent of their overall student body received special adjustments to their study situations or at examinations. Under the Norwegian government's Plan of Action for the Disabled, universities and colleges are instructed to spend 5 per cent of their maintenance funds on providing suitable conditions for students with disabilities.

Lack of appropriate experience and skills may make some staff in Norway reluctant to provide for some students with disabilities. Survey results indicated that in 1992-93 the availability of teaching aids was unsatisfactory for 20 per cent of students with disabilities receiving specially adapted further education.

Survey results for the 1989-90 year indicated that teachers of students with disabilities in upper secondary schools in Norway thought provision to be satisfactory for 70 per cent of students in ordinary classes and 82 per cent in special classes. The main changes needed were thought to be increases in time for cooperation among staff, more periods for support teaching, and improvements in technical aids. Similar general findings emerged from a 1992-93 enquiry conducted nationally by educational psychologists. There are needs for evaluation of this kind to be undertaken in further education for adults and in higher education, as little is known of the progress there of students with disabilities.

In **Spain**, there is as yet little adaptation to meet the curriculum needs of students with disabilities. The 1990 law of General Regulation of the Educational System, however, now provides a framework conducive to such adaptation.

Most further education students with disabilities in **Sweden** participate in the same programmes in upper secondary schools as do students generally. The fact that they are often termed as "integrated" or "mainstreamed", however, is indicative of the fact that despite progressive moves towards normalisation some educationalists still perceive them as not really belonging there. If schools seek modified placement for students with disabilities, the onus is on them to provide a clear justification of the necessity for this.

In the **United Kingdom**, students with disabilities can in principle have access to all further education courses, as long as they can meet course entry requirements. In addition, many colleges provide special courses for students with learning difficulties. There is a wide range of provision of further education for school leavers and for adults, although in practice access for those with disabilities varies considerably from one region to another. Generally the work focuses on those with moderate learning difficulties, although some of it is designed for those with severe learning difficulties.

The accessibility of higher education programmes to students with disabilities in the United Kingdom is not known, although in principle the universities and colleges are prepared to consider anyone who possesses the academic qualifications required for entry. There do not appear to be any adaptations to the curriculum content of existing courses to meet the needs of those with disabilities, although the development of distance learning courses has been of help. For example, during 1994-95 some 5 000 students with disabilities were enrolled on Open University courses. The existence of technical aids, including talking calculators, text telephones, radio microphones and computers, is widespread. Most institutions for higher education make special examination arrangements for students with disabilities.

In the United Kingdom, students with disabilities are thought to be particularly under-represented in science programmes and on initial teacher training courses, perhaps in part because of the health and safety issues involved. The quality of further and higher education courses is assessed by the respective national funding councils. Published inspection reports on provision in further education indicate a generally strong commitment to providing for students with disabilities but little analysis of the extent or nature of the programmes needed. Often, insufficient time is given to the co-ordination of provision across the colleges. Practice is generally more positive in vocational training than in basic classes in academic subjects.

There is a growing recognition in the United Kingdom of the need to provide pre-vocational programmes that will enable students to gain access to vocational training. Provision for those with severe learning difficulties is less well developed than that for other students with disabilities.

H. SUPPORT SERVICES

Many **Australian** universities, colleges and labour market programmes run their own support services, which include maintaining codes of practice, managing special entry arrangements, providing counselling, ensuring access, producing information booklets, transliterating materials into Braille, arranging sign language interpretation, loaning special equipment, and assisting with examinations.

The Tertiary Education Disability Council of Australia was established in 1993 to support students and its activities include publishing a national newsletter, running conferences, gathering information from disability advisers about the costs of providing support services within higher education institutions, and establishing an Internet server through which advisers can exchange information and views. The Department of Employment, Education and Training has funded a 1994-96 pilot project in which 14 regional disability liaison officers help all tertiary institutions in their regions, co-operating with disability liaison officers employed within the institutions.

Most further and higher education institutions in **British Columbia** provide a range of support services for students with disabilities, though provision in the province's four universities is generally less than that in other establishments. Typical activities include liaising with the community, modifying admission and examination arrangements, counselling, mentoring, planning physical access, and obtaining materials and equipment.

External to provision by British Columbia's further and higher education institutions are the province's Vocational Rehabilitation Services (VRS) programmes, which arrange for assessment, training, allowances, books, technical aids, and modifications to vehicles and workplaces. Through these programmes, people with disabilities are helped by rehabilitation consultants to identify realistic vocational goals and take the steps needed to achieve these goals. The VRS will liaise with the institutions to ensure that the students get access to appropriate courses and internal support services.

Within-college support services for students with disabilities in **Quebec** aim to compensate for their disabilities without conferring privileges on them, and seek to meet these aims through a personalised intervention programme.

Most vocational training institutions in **Finland** have their own student welfare services, first developed in the late 1980s, each usually co-ordinated by a student welfare group, involving the principal, the student counsellor, the physician and the nurse, and contributed to by psychologists and social workers. Only the vocational institutions specifically for students with disabilities have their own psychologist, some also employ a physiotherapist, and regular meetings of the student welfare group serve to plan and monitor individual education programmes. These special institutions are concerned with particular disabilities, offer places nationally and have contacts with the various national and local associations concerned with the same disabilities.

The National Board of Education has granted permits enabling Finland's 15 vocational institutions for students with disabilities to act as development centres, providing expertise and materials to vocational institutions running courses for students more generally and offering some places to students with disabilities, either inclusively or in special classes.

Surveyed nationally in 1995, the student welfare services in vocational training institutions in Finland were found to vary considerably, with many deficiencies in the counselling of students. Nearly half of those responding to the enquiry thought there were deficiencies, particularly in the extent of support from psychologists and social workers. The institutions' student welfare services have been affected adversely in recent years by limits on expenditure, which have resulted in larger classes and restrictions on hiring substitute teachers. Cuts have also resulted in reductions in the staffing of external support services. The development centre services started recently by the vocational institutions for students with disabilities are not yet fully established and have as yet experienced little demand.

In **Iceland**, as with further education students generally, those with disabilities have access to counsellors employed within the upper secondary schools. They also have access to external support services. The Communication Centre in Rekjavik provides sign language interpreters, the Reading Centre in the University College of Education holds courses in literacy, and the Library for the Blind produces Braille texts, tape recorded readings and computer aids. There is a Computer Centre providing advice specifically on meeting the needs of people with disabilities.

Secondary schools in **Ireland** taking on young people with disabilities are allocated support teacher time and often have the services of pastoral care staff, a teacher for special needs, a guidance counsellor and a home-school-community liaison teacher. Students without disabilities also help out. External support is provided locally through visiting teacher services for students with sensory disabilities or Down's syndrome, and there are home tuition schemes.

The Irish Department of Education runs a psychological service, which provides advice and supervises the work of guidance counsellors. The Department of Health's National Rehabilitation Board co-ordinates vocational training for people with disabilities, maintains a library on disability, publishes a quarterly journal, and provides interpreters for students with hearing or speech disabilities when they attend interviews.

Vocational training is provided for people with disabilities in Ireland by the Training and Employment Agency and by the Rehabilitation Institute. Students with disabilities seeking or receiving higher education have the support of AHEAD, which over 1996-97 is running a project designed to establish good practice in providing them with career guidance. Support is also provided through various voluntary bodies, often concerned with specific disabilities.

Within the **Italian** upper secondary schools, the main source of support for each student certificated as having a learning difficulty or disability is the support teacher assigned specifically to that student. Students generally also have recourse to the schools' counselling services. Each district also has a diagnostic and support system run by the health service, staffed by doctors, psychologists, social workers and therapists, and spending part of its time advising parents and teachers concerned with students with disabilities. Teachers may also receive support from regionally based staff of the Inspectorate, who may advise on the organisation, development and evaluation of teaching and in-service training programmes.

Among the 35 respondents to a questionnaire distributed to the 60 Italian universities in 1994, 16 stated that they provided guidance and tutoring for students with disabilities and 14 reported having a member of staff responsible for their integration.

In several counties in **Norway**, special education teams exist in the upper secondary schools, and results of a 1992-93 survey indicated that 25 per cent of the upper secondary schools sampled had a senior special education teacher in post. Most establishments engaged in vocational training employ welfare officers and doctors. In higher education, two universities have their own special advisory services for students with disabilities, helping students overcome difficulties in mobility, hearing, vision and literacy, and each of these universities has a Council for Disabled Students.

Further education students in Norway, whether they are in upper secondary school programmes, vocational training schemes or adult education provision, have access to the municipalities' educational psychological services, offering expertise in psychology, in disability and in social education. Those in the 16 to 19 age group also have access to county-based multi-disciplinary follow-up services, designed to help young people during their period of transition from compulsory schooling to higher education or to employment.

In Norway people of any age, if they have disabilities, can draw on the services of the national resource centres for special education. There are 20 altogether, former special schools, with a total staffing of some 1 300, and each providing expertise and guidance relevant to a particular kind of disability. Dispersed around the country there are special teachers for the hearing impaired and for the visually impaired. A recent development at county level is that of inter-disciplinary habilitation teams, who work with children and adults who have severe learning difficulties. Some counties have technical aid centres and all have employment counselling services. There have been notable attempts to co-ordinate services across the education, health and social welfare agencies.

Support services external to the institutions for further and higher education in **Spain** are provided through voluntary organisations, which are concerned with various disabilities and which receive funding from the Ministry for Social Affairs. This ministry also runs a State Centre for Personal Autonomy and Technical Aids. While the activities and professionalism of voluntary agencies concerned with disabilities are increasing, the provision of services is geographically uneven, with large cities rather better served than other areas.

The **Swedish** Agency for Special Education is a government agency which distributes funds nationally for certain special education programmes. Through its 27 regional bases it provides a support service for teachers, for parents, and for students with disabilities, offering advice on special education and developing relevant materials.

Staffing of the Swedish Agency for Special Education's bases includes advisers specialising in aspects such as visual impairment, physical handicap, and the needs of immigrant students with disabilities. Each of the country's four educational materials centres specialises in a different disability: physical, visual, auditory and severe learning difficulties. For example, the services of the centre for visual impairment include translating teaching materials into Braille, on request, for individual teachers. There is also a unit which co-ordinates the distribution of computer programmes. One of the functions of the Swedish Agency for Special Education is to evaluate the adapted learning materials produced by its regional educational materials centres.

In the **United Kingdom**, many of the colleges providing further education have their own support services for students with disabilities. The national system of funding encourages them to do this, by allocating extra allowances to meet the extra costs of educating students demonstrably in need of additional teaching, interpretation or welfare support.

Most of the colleges of further education in the United Kingdom also rely on external support for services such as transport, welfare funding, advice from educational psychologists, careers guidance, speech therapy, and the loan of specialised equipment for students with auditory or visual impairment. The Training and Enterprise Council, through its funding and monitoring of individual training plans, carries a responsibility for ensuring that the support needs of trainees with disabilities are met.

There are many nationally operating voluntary bodies concerned with disability in the United Kingdom, mostly providing support services both for children and for adults, and mostly focusing on specific disabilities. One, entitled "Skill", is concerned specifically with students with disabilities, whatever the nature of the disability, at the levels both of further and of higher education. There is also the government-sponsored National Advisory Council on the Employment of People with Disabilities, which carries training as part of its brief.

Support services for students with disabilities within the United Kingdom's higher education institutions are wide ranging. They include note-taking, interpretation into sign language, transcription into Braille, help with study skills, and provision of computers, tape recorders, screens with large print format, and machines which read books out loud. Some institutions have set up mentoring schemes whereby existing students with disabilities help new entrants.

In the United Kingdom, the effectiveness of support services run within colleges of further education for students with disabilities is monitored through the Further Education Funding Council's inspection procedures. Evidence indicates that support is mainly through the students' periodic attendance at the colleges' special workshops or resource centres. The support provided there is good in meeting students' physical needs but tends to lack specific objectives and to be insufficiently well linked with their ordinary vocational programmes. When the students are helped in ordinary classrooms, too often the teaching strategies used prevent them from playing an active part in the whole class lessons.

The extent of within-institution support services for students with disabilities varies considerably across the United Kingdom's higher education institutions. Appropriate services do exist generally, but the extent to which each institution meets each student's needs is not known. Characteristics of a successful service are likely to be integration within the institution's senior management structure and a visible and accessible centrally placed location. Support units have been established in some higher education institutions as part of a government initiative, with the condition that they provide formal written reports of their monitoring procedures, and some have engaged people from other institutions to assess progress.

I.   INFORMATION TECHNOLOGY

In **Australia** the Open Training and Education Network is a New South Wales initiative, producing 100 hours of satellite broadcasting in 1994 for the 25 000 college students and 3 500 high school students then on roll. Its 700 staff design and develop educational resource materials, mount distance delivery courses, manage the broadcasting service and run a library network. The Queensland-based Tertiary Initiatives for People with Disabilities Outreach Program operates through the Internet and helps students with disabilities use electronic mail to link with one another and with staff of universities and secondary schools.

The majority of tertiary institutions and public libraries in Australia run information technology services for people with disabilities. Available equipment includes speech synthesisers, ergonomic furniture, talking book machines, talking typewriters, Braille computer terminals, print enhancers, automatic page turners, and equipment for converting between speech, text and Braille. The near future is likely to see the development of telecommunications platforms, which will integrate services such as broadcast television, pay television, face to face tutorials, computer conferencing, electronic mail, bulletin boards, and library resources.

As part of **British Columbia**'s Vocational Rehabilitation Services (VRS) provision, a Vancouver-based special education technology project offers on a province-wide basis a service whereby people with disabilities are helped to identify the technological skills they need to achieve their vocational goals, borrow adaptive technology and software, receive training in their use, and have their borrowed equipment maintained and repaired.

The colleges serving as centres of excellence with respect to students with disabilities in **Quebec** were helped exercise their roles through grants for technological equipment, for example for use in producing documents in Braille or for lending to other colleges. As stocks increase, it should be possible for a more mobile collection to be established. Individuals can apply to various government schemes for equipment for personal use; for example, they may be able to obtain a grant from the Quebec Office for the Disabled.

The vocational institutions in **Finland** have good information technology facilities for students generally, and there is in existence enough software designed to meet students' special needs, but it is only in the institutions specialising in social and vocational training for students with disabilities that there is sufficient special education equipment. Some teachers still lack the skills needed to incorporate information technology into their teaching. The University of Jyväskylä and several vocational institutions, folk high schools and municipal authority welfare services are involved in projects developing multimedia teaching programmes and distance learning networks for people with disabilities.

In **Iceland**, the hardware and software needed in further education are provided by the upper secondary schools, and there is a Computer Centre for the Handicapped that provides advice to the institutions.

Post-compulsory education students in secondary schools in **Ireland** have good access to computers and associated courses, and many schools offer extra opportunities to help them carry out their school work and to enhance their later employability. The Department of Education provides equipment grants for those whose disabilities prevent them from communicating through speech or handwriting.

Special education has been given some priority in the development of information technology in **Norway** and numerous projects have been carried out. Recommendations to Parliament in 1993-94 included increased use of information technology in curricula, the creation of computer networks, the establishment of a national database to catalogue existing special education software, the adaptation of standard software for use by people with disabilities, and the development of distance learning. The special education competence centres are currently building up expertise in information technology and a distance learning project has been established to provide advice for educational psychologists and for teachers. The technical aid centres lend data equipment but do not as yet provide instruction in its use.

In **Spain** the Ministry of Science and Education has established an information technology service, with one of the service's departments developing and promulgating software for helping pupils and students with disabilities. For example, there is a computer-aided programme on speech therapy. The State Centre for Personal Autonomy and Technical Aids, run by the Ministry for Social Affairs, also carries many applications of information technology.

The **Swedish** Agency for Special Education's unit for computer instruction provides expertise in the use of computers with and by students with disabilities and supports the regional computer resource centres. It helps the centres to employ people who have expertise in teaching, in special education and in computing, and who on this basis support teachers and students in the schools.

In the **United Kingdom**, while there have been many government-sponsored developments over the past decade in the uses of information technology with and by children of statutory school age, there has not been the same consistency of central support in post-compulsory education, and developments there have been patchy. The most notable successes have been in helping able students with physical disability or visual impairment to gain access to institutions' mainstream curriculum.

Currently in the United Kingdom there are several projects developing uses of information technology in improving opportunities for students with disabilities to learn. One, for example, has been to set up a database, available through the Joint Academic Network (JANET), which now provides a forum for support workers in the field of disability to discuss possible information technology solutions to learning problems experienced by their clients. Projects are also planned to make JANET directly accessible to people with disabilities, thus helping them to solve their own problems. Another project aims to help students with literacy difficulties to use computer software to by-pass their problems, for example by using programmes mediating between speech and writing.

Future developments envisaged in the United Kingdom and likely to help students with disabilities include greatly enhanced transmission of information, not only in text form but also in recorded sound and moving pictures, between homes, community centres, libraries, educational institutions and broadcasting companies. As the Internet becomes more widespread and as digital broadcasting develops, there should be increasing opportunities for people with minority interests and needs, including those with disabilities, to be catered for.

J. TEACHER TRAINING

Most teachers in post-compulsory education in **Australia** see themselves primarily as subject specialists and have received little initial training in working with students with disabilities. The availability of in-service training is, however, increasing, and most college staff have now been involved in at least the first level of awareness raising activities. Some of the government-initiated National Professional Development Projects focus on specific disability groups. Queensland's AccessA*bility* project includes a nationally available training kit for staff in further and higher education. At national level the competency-based ResponseA*bility* programme and the FlexA*bility* programme both provide training for work with students with disabilities in vocational training schemes. Various universities run degree level and diploma level courses in disability studies.

Most further and higher education establishments in **British Columbia** provide some form of in-service training in teaching students with disabilities. Typical activities include general awareness initiatives and workshops for staff and students concerning more particular disability issues.

Responsibilities of colleges in **Quebec** for co-ordinating services for their students with disabilities include raising awareness of staff and of members of the community concerning these students' needs and helping staff to adjust their teaching to meet these needs.

Whereas all those undertaking initial training to teach on vocational courses generally in **Finland** used to attend a 20-hour element on disabilities, this is now just an option. Individual differences, however, are considered throughout the training. Various short-term courses in special education are run by the National Board of Education, by universities, by teacher training institutes and by associations concerned with particular disabilities. While most are mainly for staff of schools, they are often of some relevance to further education and some focus on vocational training.

Training specifically to teach students with disabilities on vocational courses has been in existence in Finland since the 1970s and by 1995 about 500 people had received this training. It is undertaken by teachers who have already undertaken the general training and have had some experience of teaching on vocational courses. About half of these trainees have already worked in vocational institutions providing specifically for students with disabilities. Each trainee is helped to devise and follow a personal development plan, in which the individualisation of teaching is likely to feature strongly. Since 1993, the Jyväskylä Vocational Teacher Training Institute has been running a course, currently taking 19 trainees, providing training in teaching adults with severe learning difficulties.

In **Iceland**, teachers are trained through one-year postgraduate certificate courses, which include a special education element.

Teachers providing post-compulsory education in **Ireland** are not required to have undertaken any training in special education, although some initial teacher training programmes include an optional module on disability awareness. Following initial training and three or more years of teaching experience, a few have completed a one-year in-service course leading to a certificate or a higher diploma in special education. Some teachers have undertaken in-service training in pastoral care. Guidance counsellors, special education co-ordinators and visiting teachers providing support services to meet special needs have all received training in their respective fields.

Support teachers working with students certificated as having learning difficulties or disabilities in **Italy** have to undertake further training. This is organised at regional level, is monitored by the country's Inspectorate, and is taken over a two-year period. Much of it consists of on-the-job training. The course includes the study of psychology, teaching methods, and relevant legislation. The teacher is trained to act as a researcher in undertaking support teaching and completes a thesis, which the candidate has to discuss before a commission including inspectors from outside the region.

In **Norway**, in 1988, only 8.8 per cent of teachers in upper secondary schools had undergone a year or more of training in special education. Subsequently, extensive opportunities have been made available for such training and by 1993, 55 per cent of the teachers in these schools had completed this training. The proportion of teachers and trainers with this training in adult education and in work preparation schemes is not known, however, and it is thought that there is virtually no such expertise in higher education.

Most of **Spain**'s 170 resource centres for teachers provide expert advice, materials and in-service training with respect to special educational needs, although only a small proportion of the service thus provided is directly relevant to further education and the teaching of students with disabilities in higher education is not represented. There are university postgraduate courses in special education but again these are focused on work with children rather than on work with students in post-compulsory education.

Initial training for ordinary teaching in **Sweden** includes a total of 10 weeks in which students learn about some of the broader issues in special education. Some qualified teachers follow a 1.5-year university course on special education. They then work in an advisory capacity within their own municipalities, but are unlikely to have expertise in helping students with severe learning difficulties.

Advisers employed by the Swedish Agency for Special Education have an average of 10 years of teaching experience and more than 90 per cent of them have postgraduate degrees in special education.

In the **United Kingdom**, teachers working in post-compulsory education are not required to undertake formal teacher training, though many do, usually through two-year part-time courses followed while already employed as teachers. In undertaking this training they are usually paid for through staff development funds administered by the institutions in which they are working. However, few of the staff working with students who have disabilities possess any qualifications in the field of special education. Most of the training in special education provided by institutions occurs in colleges of further education, not in higher education institutions, and most of it consists of raising awareness rather than of improving methods of curriculum modification.

K.   COMMUNITY INVOLVEMENT

Parents, relevant community personnel and service providers in **Australia** are actively involved in planning for the successful transition of students with disabilities from one phase of their education and training to the next. While some of this involvement is at an informal level, there are 20 community-based transition teams in operation.

The Australian National Training Authority agreement of 1992 has provided the basis for many partnerships between schools, vocational training establishments and industry. As part of these partnerships, vocational courses train students to develop competencies that meet recognised industrial standards. The government's Partnerships with Industry Initiative creates links between corporations willing to employ people with disabilities and the Service Placement and Training agencies.

Whereas co-operation between home and school has a significant part to play in education in **Finland**, links of this kind are not established in vocational training. Voluntary work does not make a formal contribution to the further education of students with disabilities and the extent to which it occurs informally is not known nationally. Community attitudes towards disability are neutral and one is unlikely to come across expressions of hostility. The media publicise disability issues to some extent, generally in positive terms.

In **Iceland**, voluntary organisations such as women's clubs, Rotary clubs and The Lions sometimes collect money to give to organisations concerned specifically with disabilities.

Voluntary bodies in **Ireland** are usually concerned with particular disabilities, as are associations of parents. In addition to involvement in the provision of services for children and adults with disabilities, they are active in providing advice about available services and equipment, in running workshops and conferences, and in advocating treatment. The National Association for the Deaf, for example, has set up a communication training scheme and a technical equipment demonstration centre, and the National Council for the Blind provides a Brailling service.

Within each province in **Italy**, the head teachers and teachers in the upper secondary schools are directly responsible to the Provincial Director of Education, who consults with the Provincial Schools Council, which includes parent representation. Parents are also represented on the district schools councils, as are students, trade union members and people with local economic and cultural interests. In addition, they are represented on each individual School Council.

In **Norway**, different groups of people with disabilities are served by a large number of voluntary organisations, which receive financial support from the government and which make an important supplementary contribution to education and training in the public sector.

Much of the effort in **Spain** to involve the general community in consideration of the needs of students with disabilities comes from voluntary organisations where membership consists mainly of representatives of families which include a person with a disability.

In the **United Kingdom**, colleges of further education are required by their funding council to draw up strategic plans, and in doing so are encouraged to identify and respond to local community needs. The Further Education Funding Council's nine regional committees, as well as having business and educational representatives, each have at least one member with a special interest in the education of people with disabilities. They keep regional facilities under review, with one of their specific remits relating to disability, and advise on changes needed. At a more local level, inclusion of community representatives on the governing bodies of colleges helps to ensure that community interests are looked after. Similarly, local community interests are represented on the management boards of the Training and Enterprise Councils.

L. POST-EDUCATION EXPERIENCE

The emphasis in **Australia** has been on increasing participation rates in higher education, and results of these increases, in terms of employment, are only just beginning to emerge. Among students with disabilities graduating from the University of Queensland in 1991, 18 per cent continued with their studies (as opposed to 26 per cent of all graduates), 60 per cent found employment (66 per cent for the total cohort) and 11 per cent were unemployed and seeking work (5 per cent for the total). Figures for 1992 were similar.

Cost-benefit analysis undertaken in **Quebec** has demonstrated the effectiveness of post-compulsory education for students with disabilities in reducing their dependence on social assistance schemes on leaving education.

Finding employment after vocational training is difficult for young people generally in **Finland** and particularly so for those with disabilities. (The 1995 edition of OECD *in Figures* indicated that Finland had one of the highest unemployment rates among Member countries, running at 18 per cent.) Although there have been follow-up studies of students completing vocational training generally, the statistics generated do not identify the outcomes for those with disabilities. Studies of outcomes for those recently leaving vocational institutions providing specifically for students with disabilities yield unemployment rates averaging 23 per cent.

In recent years there has been some development in Finland of arrangements for open sheltered work, whereby people are given work which is located in ordinary work places but which does not carry benefits such as an employment contract or relevant salary. Several vocational institutions providing specifically for students with disabilities are now participating in supported employment projects, which exist throughout the country. Staff in these institutions are responsible for following their trainees through into independent living and employment where possible, and there is a need for staff in the vocational institutions for students generally to take on similar responsibilities, particularly with respect to the increasing number of students with disabilities there.

In **Iceland**, people with disabilities have, in principle, the same access to post-educational opportunities as do others.

In the **Netherlands**, the Social and Cultural Planning Bureau reported in 1996 that participation in the labour market for people with serious disabilities was only half that to be expected on the basis of demographic data and estimated that at least 50 per cent of the students with impairments not completing secondary education would never enter the labour market, remaining dependent on government support. This places pressure on other facilities. For example, while some 80 000 people with mental handicap were attending sheltered workshops in 1995, waiting lists for such places, which had stood at 12 000 in 1992, were growing.

The results of **Norwegian** surveys concerned with the living conditions of people with disabilities indicate that, by comparison with those without disabilities, they participate less in working life, they are more likely to leave jobs through lack of suitable conditions, they take more sick leave, their educational attainments are lower, their incomes are lower, they often live alone or with their parents, they have higher living expenses, and they have difficulties in joining clubs and in participating in open-air activities. The government tries to offset some of these problems by subsidising employers and intends, in addition, to try out quota arrangements, whereby a certain percentage of people employed in organisations have disabilities.

Although there has been much progress over the past 15 years in **Spain**, the quality of life for people with disabilities is reported to be still far from what it should be.

Following their participation in the **United Kingdom**'s 1993-94 Youth Training and Training for Work programmes, the percentages of those with disabilities gaining a qualification (48 per cent and 39 per cent respectively) were on a par with the percentages of participants overall. Percentages finding work, however, (40 per cent and 28 per cent respectively) were lower than those overall (53 per cent and 35 per cent respectively).

M. WAYS FORWARD

In **Australia**, while participation rates for students with disabilities are still too low, there have been promising developments within the National Training Reform Agenda. One of the greatest needs is that for financial support. Disability allowances do not appear to cover the costs and should be reviewed with a view to individual targeting. While gains have been made through the use of techno-logical resources, there is a need for further development to be set within a policy framework. There has been progress with respect to institutions' entrance require-ments, attitudes, teaching methods and assessment processes, but more is needed. A national code of practice and associated staff development pro-grammes could increase the likelihood of their happening.

One of the key issues identified in **British Columbia** is the need for the further development of support services. Institutions vary, with the universities offering less than the colleges. Generally, there are needs for more interpreting for students with hearing impairment, more tutoring for those with severe learning disabilities, and more brailled materials for those with visual impairment. Provi-sion of technical aids is extensive but requires more effective co-ordination. Attitudinal barriers still exist, and staff generally need more expertise in special education. The costs of the assessment needed to provide documentary evi-dence of disability are excessive.

In **Quebec**, much has been done over the past 15 years to make college education accessible to people with disabilities, notably in establishing two col-leges as centres of excellence and then disseminating the expertise gained across colleges more generally. Next steps are to continue information campaigns in the community and to ensure that colleges now taking on more active supporting roles with respect to students with disabilities maintain their commitment.

In recent years the increase in the extent to which vocational training is open to young people with disabilities in **Finland** has been considerable. However, the institutions offering vocational training for students generally have not yet acquired the knowledge, skills and attitudes needed to provide effectively for the increasing number of students with disabilities on roll. There is a need for the systematic training of staff. Networking arrangements across institutions could help in the dissemination of expertise. While institutions providing specifically for students with disabilities are beginning to act as development centres, they need to clarify their roles and market their services.

Arrangements to enhance transition of students in Finland from one stage of education and training to the next exist but are in need of improvement. Vocational training for students with disabilities is still focused on a relatively narrow range of activity. It needs to be broadened, to become more versatile, and to be more closely linked with working life. Now that decentralisation has reduced the role of the National Board of Education, the vocational training institutions must take on their increased responsibilities for organising their activities, monitoring their effectiveness, developing in-service training for their teachers, and providing the support services needed.

In **Iceland**, much has been gained by the fact that further education in the upper secondary school is, by law, open to all. For students with disabilities, some good curriculum development has occurred. The next step is to try to ensure that all upper secondary schools want to make this a reality. A bill currently before Parliament, requiring all ordinary upper secondary schools to make appropriate provision for students with disabilities, should result in further progress in this direction.

In **Ireland**, the Department of Education has statutory responsibility for providing education and co-ordinating support services for all the region's students with disabilities, who will be registered as such on a national database. In line with current integration policy, existing special schools will act as resource centres and where feasible students with disabilities will have the choice of attending ordinary schools with access to support services based in special schools. With regard to students with disabilities, schools will have written policies and plans, curriculum development projects will be established nationally and teachers will have appropriate in-service training.

In **Norway**, the objectives of normalising services and integrating people with disabilities into ordinary education and training schemes have to a large extent been achieved. In further education, 60 per cent of students with disabilities attend ordinary classes and very few, mostly those with hearing impairment, go to special education institutions. There is an extensive network of advisory services.

There is some doubt, however, as to whether the Norwegian teachers and trainers helping students with disabilities have sufficient expertise in special education to make full use of the resources at their disposal. Because of the normalisation of services, many of those with disabilities have difficulty in finding out about their rights and in getting access to the services to which they are entitled. It is important to ensure that they have full access to further education, for example, and that any qualifications they obtain are fully documented and are fully recognised by employers and by educationalists.

In **Spain**, one priority for the future is an improvement in the training of teachers for work with students with disabilities. There is also a need both to extend and to co-ordinate existing services.

In the **United Kingdom**, one notably successful development has been the Further Education Funding council's strategy of funding colleges on a recurrent basis, with its requirements that the colleges declare their teaching objectives and outcomes being supported by the council's arrangements for periodic inspection. This has had a significant positive impact on the quality and range of opportunities for further education students with learning difficulties and/or disabilities.

Notwithstanding the gains experienced in the United Kingdom in the further education of students with disabilities, there is thought to be room for further improvement, particularly in teachers' abilities to tailor programmes to meet individual needs and to identify outcomes. There is also a need for improved inter-agency collaboration at local level, and the government is in the process of issuing guidance in this field, including examples of good practice. Other initiatives planned by the government, both in further and in higher education, aim at improving access for people with disabilities to education and training programmes, and at helping them develop their self-esteem and work in mainstream settings where possible.

PARTICIPANTS OF THE WORKING GROUP

Edward Brittain   Further Education Support Unit, Department for Education and Employment, London, United Kingdom.

Peter Evans   OECD/CERI Secretariat; Head of the Study of Effective Education and Support Structures for Students with Disabilities in Integrated Settings.

Don Labon   Senior Consultant to the CERI study; author of the report.

Ray Miner   Deputy Director, Division of Educational Services, Department of Education, Washington DC, United States.

Solveig Reindal   Professor of Special Education, University of Oslo, Norway.

Annex 2

NOTES OF GUIDANCE FOR COMPLETION
OF THE COUNTRY QUESTIONNAIRES

PART ONE

A. Main characteristics of post-compulsory education

There should be a description of the ways in which opportunities are structured: the different levels and types of education and training on offer; the establishments within which they occur; the entry requirements; the funding arrangements. There should also be some reference to numbers and age ranges of full-time and part-time students and trainees, along with an indication of the proportion of the total population being provided for in the main age groups being served. There should be some indication of the goals of each form of provision: qualifications being obtained, vocations or other lifestyles being prepared for.

There should also be some reference to the training of teachers for work in the field of post-compulsory education and training: an indication of the nature of such teacher training, distinguishing between theoretical and practical elements; if this training is not mandatory, an estimate of the proportion of teachers who have undertaken it, identifying any differences with respect to the different kinds of establishment in which they work.

B. The population under consideration

The focus is on the first decade following compulsory schooling (in most countries, 16 to 26 years old). However, if their available statistics permit an extension of this, country representatives are invited to make some additional reference to education and training for older age groups. While the post-compulsory range is that beyond the age range during which school attendance is compulsory, it may include an initial period during which education authorities are obliged to make provision for those who wish to make use of it. In some circumstances the obligation may be to provide for students with disabilities but not for students generally.

The population under consideration is not simply an upward extension of that with which the school-level elements of the study are concerned. Some children with disabilities, notably many of those with relatively mild learning and/or adjustment difficulties, will leave school not wishing to participate in any further education and indeed may not require it. If they do, the flexibility and diversity of post-school opportunities for education and training may be such that they can participate and succeed without requiring any adaptations to the curriculum on offer more generally. Comparison of these two populations is also complicated by the fact that definitions of disability vary from one country to another. Furthermore, some children recover from their disabilities, some do not survive to adulthood and some people acquire disabilities, for example through teenage motor accidents.

There should be some definition of the term "disability" as used in the country report, perhaps through descriptions of the kinds and degrees of disability included. The prevalence of the population under consideration should be quantified as far as possible, for example as a percentage of the total population. If prevalence varies from one age group to another, it may be possible to provide some indication of the nature of this variation. Furthermore, some indication of variation in prevalence from one disability to another should be possible. If differing estimates appear in statistics from different sources, for example from education, health and welfare agencies, it may be necessary to provide some indication of the uncertainties they introduce.

C. Policies and legislation

Government policy concerning disability may be international in the sense that there is explicit recognition of the country's having accepted the responsibilities involved in signing formal declarations such as those adopted by the General Assembly of the United Nations. National policy may emanate from departments other than that of education; it may be a product of inter-departmental agreement, following consultation across education, health and welfare agencies. If there are important regional or district variations in policy, these should be mentioned.

There will probably be some legislative framework governing the opportunities which those with disabilities have for post-school education, training and employment. Policy and legislation may be with respect to particular age bands only. Legislation may be mandatory, advisory or conditional on certain circumstances, such as lack of financial resources. As with policy, legislation may stem from more than one government department.

D. Transition from schooling

Placement beyond school may be undertaken following a formal review of progress, perhaps involving psychological or multi-disciplinary assessment. If selection procedures are involved, students may or may not be allowed to compensate for difficulties, for example by having questions read out to them or recorded on audiotape if they have visual impairment or if they have specific difficulties in literacy acquisition.

Ordinary schools and special schools may well differ in the extent to which they facilitate smooth transition of students with disabilities to appropriate tertiary education establishments and workplaces, as may day schools and residential schools, and the situation may be better for students with some kinds of disability than it is for others. Some vocational courses may start prior to school leaving and continue thereafter.

Liaison may include visits to schools from tertiary educators or employers, opportunities for school leavers to make preliminary visits to likely placements, and arrangements for careers officers and other advisers to have interviews with individual students and their parents. Students with disabilities may be involved in the same transition arrangements as are students without disabilities, or they may have special separate arrangements; either way, what is on offer may or may not be helpful.

Country reports should indicate the kinds of transition arrangement in existence, identify good practice and estimate the extent to which it exists.

E. Funding

Funding may be at national or at local level, and may come from a variety of sources; state education, health and welfare agencies may all be involved in one way or another, and voluntary bodies may contribute too. There may be some diverting of funds within the establishments themselves. Allocations may be on a block basis or with respect to individual students or trainees. They may favour some disabilities as opposed to others. They may be for specific resources, such as computers, hearing aids, Braille texts, or recording equipment. Awards may be subject to age limits. While carrying some advantages, they may be presented in ways that stigmatise the recipients. They may favour some kinds of provision; for example, colleges may be able to obtain extra funding for students attending separate special education classes but not for the same students if they are integrated into ordinary classes.

Financial limitations may reduce people's opportunities to avail themselves of education and training on offer. This section of the report should include some assessment of the extent to which disability allowances and other kinds of financial support enable people with disabilities to meet the costs of the provision they need.

F. Provision

In providing statistical information, the country report should indicate the age ranges involved, particularly where the figures gathered have been for some ages only. It may be possible to provide a breakdown, for example by stating numbers in the 16 to 26 age range and numbers aged 27 or more. If a more detailed breakdown with respect to age is feasible (the more detailed the better), perhaps tables can be added as annexes.

Restrictions may be with respect to school leaving qualifications, to performance on entry examinations or psychological tests, or to levels of independence and physical mobility. Restrictions will not necessarily be made explicit by the providers, and they may reflect limitations in the buildings and their facilities rather than curriculum requirements as such.

There should be some indication, quantified as far as possible, of the extent to which the various forms of provision available meet the educational and training needs of those with disabilities. There should be some reference to establishments' policies concerning those with disabilities. Information on the extent to which establishments monitor and evaluate their facilities for those with disabilities would be of interest. If there are variations across regions, across age groups or across disabilities it will be helpful if these are stated. It may be that educational and training needs can be met through existing provision but that overall needs would be met better if there were alternative offerings. For example, it may be that provision for the blind exists on a residential basis but that some blind students could fare better if it were offered on a day basis as well.

G. The curriculum

This section is concerned with the content of the programmes available to students and trainees with disabilities, with the appropriateness of the teaching resources and methods used, and with the benefits the programmes confer on those completing them. Some distinction will need to be made between programmes that were designed specifically for students or trainees with disabilities in segregated settings and programmes that were designed for people more generally and then perhaps modified to make them accessible to those entrants who happened to have disabilities.

Taking into account the limits imposed by students' competences, some indication should be given of the range of courses available to students with disabilities and of the extent to which this may fall short of the range available to students without disabilities. For example, it may be that students with physical disabilities have good access to courses providing training in the use of computers, because they may then be able to do computer work from home, but that those with interests and aptitude in engineering are discouraged from taking such courses, on the grounds that they would not be welcomed in workshops even if they were to gain the appropriate qualifications. Similarly, effective modification of one programme for the benefit of students with disabilities may reduce the likelihood of those students being offered places on other programmes.

If possible the report should include any evidence of the use of special teaching materials and methods designed to enable students with disabilities to participate, together with some indication of the prevalence of such practices. Adapted materials might include texts transposed into Braille, translations of texts originally published in foreign languages, sound recordings of lectures, subtitled video programmes, simplified written introductions to new topics, laboratory and workshop equipment designed to make few demands on manual dexterity, and computers with modified keyboards or enlarged display units. Methods might include the use of sign language and the running of extra seminars and tutorials for students experiencing difficulties.

Insofar as students with disabilities do not have full access to the curriculum this section may be able to provide some assessment of the extent to which shortfalls are due to factors such as teachers' attitudes, their lack of knowledge or skills, shortages in number of staff, or limitations in equipment. If the report judges that students with disabilities should have greater curriculum access, it may be able to go on to say something about ways in which the situation can be improved.

There should be some reference to the relationships between the curriculum and participants' lives outside these programmes, particularly when they receive education and training on a part-time basis. For example, courses may or may not have relevance to their part-time employment, to their leisure interests, and to their developing independence at home or in residential care. If such links do not exist, the question arises as to the steps which the providers may take to increase their awareness of students' and trainees' lives more generally.

There should be some reference to ways in which the successes of students with disabilities on these programmes are assessed, whether any modifications are needed in the interests of fair and accurate assessment, and whether such modifications as are carried out are appropriate. Modifications may include, for example, provision of computers with modified keyboards and of people to transcribe oral responses to examination questions.

This section should also comment on the effectiveness of establishments' methods of quality control, for example through analysis of completion rates, through the gathering of participants' views, and through the commentaries of internal and external examiners. There should also be some overall judgement as to the extent to which successful completion of programmes is of benefit to the students and trainees.

H. Support services

This section is concerned not only with support provided by people based within the educational and training establishments identified but also with support provided by organisations outside these establishments. There should be some judgement as to the extent to which these services meet students' and trainees' needs for support, and some judgement as to the extent to which internal and external support services are effectively and efficiently co-ordinated, both in themselves and in relation to each other.

Internal support services may be provided by groups of students and trainees with or without disabilities, by staff of the establishments generally or by staff appointed specially for this purpose. Specialist staff may include counsellors or welfare officers with assigned responsibilities for all students and trainees or solely for those with disabilities.

External support service staff may work with the student or trainee, with the family, with teachers, with support service staff based within the establishment, and with support service staff employed by different agencies. Support services may be provided by education, health, social or welfare agencies, or by voluntary bodies. Some support service staff, for example those employed by societies for the blind or deaf, will be concerned with only one kind of disability.

Support service staff may be involved in teaching as well as in assessing and advising, some will offer in-service training in ways of helping students and trainees with disabilities, and some may be required to monitor, inspect and evaluate provision. Some groups, for example local clubs with philanthropic functions, may on occasion provide support for people with disabilities by engaging in fund-raising activities.

This section should provide some indication of the extent to which internal and external support services are evaluated, either within themselves or collectively, together with a view concerning the effectiveness of such evaluation and a comment on its outcomes. As before, this section of the report should be quantified as far as possible and should be sensitive to any variations with regard to regions, age bands and disabilities. It may be able to assess whether any gains in efficiency and effectiveness might be made through re-organisation, for example through a shifting of emphasis from external to internal support services or vice versa.

I. Information technology

This section should assess the extent to which current advances in information technology are being used for the benefit of students and trainees with disabilities, and should estimate the extent to which their potential is likely to be realised with respect to these students in the near future. Possibilities include robotic devices that can help people compensate for their physical disabilities, computer simulations of situations to which people's disabilities prevent them from having direct access, and modems connecting computers with electronic data networks.

J. Teacher training

Insofar as initial training for teaching in post-compulsory education and training exists, in this section there should be quantified reference to any attempts to familiarise trainee teachers with disability issues and to help them to develop materials and methods needed to teach students with disabilities. If any of these courses contain substantial options devoted specifically to teaching students with disabilities, this section could well refer to them. Similarly, any initial courses designed specifically to train people to teach students with disabilities should be described.

Existing teachers in post-compulsory education and training may have access to in-service training programmes designed to help them work with students with disabilities. The people running these programmes may be special education specialists in the same establishments, or they may work in external support services run by district or regional education authorities or teacher training institutions.

The programmes may vary in duration and they may or may not lead to qualifications. They may be designed to influence attitudes, to aid awareness of disability issues, to increase knowledge, or to develop skills. Where such programmes exist, this section should indicate their prevalence, nature, duration, and the extent to which they meet teachers' needs. If advanced courses in teaching students with disabilities exist, they too should be identified.

Wherever teacher training courses are described, if some reference can be made to their quality, so much the better.

K. Community involvement

Any community support for students with disabilities provided by local or national voluntary organisations will have been described in the section on support services. There are, however, other forms of community involvement that may be referred to here.

Students and trainees with disabilities are likely to have the continuing support of their parents and perhaps of other relatives. Individuals may provide voluntary help, members of the community may represent the interests of students with disabilities on the governing bodies of education establishments, and teachers or managers may arrange to consult regularly with parents or other carers of students with disabilities who cannot be fully independent. Staff of establishments may run awareness courses on disability and invite members of the community to participate. Individuals may agree to serve as advocates for particular students with disabilities, and on this basis it may be they who take the initiative in discussing education and training issues with staff of teaching or workplace establishments.

As in earlier sections, data reported should be quantified as far as possible, to give the reader some idea of the prevalence of the practices referred to and of the extent to which communities are influenced by them.

L. Post-education experience

Post-compulsory education and training can be considered as ideally constituting a life-long experience, whereby many school leavers enter a stage of full-time higher education or vocational training and thereafter combine employment with periodic part-time participation in education and training for vocational or leisure purposes. While not part of the main focus of the report, some reference to the experiences of people with disabilities once they leave full-time education and training would be helpful.

It would be useful to know whether providers of post-compulsory education and training undertake follow-up studies, the extent to which they have been successful in preparing people with disabilities for the labour market or for more generally fulfilled lives, and whether further steps should be taken in trying to ensure that people with disabilities obtain appropriate employment.

M. Ways forward

This final section should summarise the country's most promising developments, identify any major shortfalls and suggest steps through which limitations might be overcome. Some indication of the rate at which provision is changing and of the direction in which it is moving would be helpful.

PART TWO: SYNTHESIS OF COUNTRY REPORTS

Each case study report should be of up to five pages in length and should follow broadly the same structure as the country report, but with respect to a single establishment or programme. In most cases it should be possible to use the same section headings. Thus there will be an introductory outline of the establishment's overall structure, clientele and goals, followed by sections on the number and kinds of students or trainees with disabilities provided for, on the establishment's policies and regulations with respect to those with disabilities, on arrangements facilitating their transition from schooling, on funding issues, on available forms of provision and their entry requirements, on curriculum modifications, on internal and external support services, on uses of information technology, on teacher training, on community involvement, on the destinations of leavers, and on possibilities for further development.

As with the country reports the case studies should be evaluative as well as descriptive. The emphasis should be on providing examples of good practice that can be used, without naming the establishments concerned, to illustrate aspects of the composite report.

MAIN SALES OUTLETS OF OECD PUBLICATIONS
PRINCIPAUX POINTS DE VENTE DES PUBLICATIONS DE L'OCDE

AUSTRALIA – AUSTRALIE
D.A. Information Services
648 Whitehorse Road, P.O.B 163
Mitcham, Victoria 3132   Tel. (03) 9210.7777
Fax: (03) 9210.7788

AUSTRIA – AUTRICHE
Gerold & Co.
Graben 31
Wien I   Tel. (0222) 533.50.14
Fax: (0222) 512.47.31.29

BELGIUM – BELGIQUE
Jean De Lannoy
Avenue du Roi, Koningslaan 202
B-1060 Bruxelles Tel. (02) 538.51.69/538.08.41
Fax: (02) 538.08.41

CANADA
Renouf Publishing Company Ltd.
5369 Canotek Road
Unit 1
Ottawa, Ont. K1J 9J3   Tel. (613) 745.2665
Fax: (613) 745.7660

Stores:
71 1/2 Sparks Street
Ottawa, Ont. K1P 5R1   Tel. (613) 238.8985
Fax: (613) 238.6041

12 Adelaide Street West
Toronto, QN M5H 1L6   Tel. (416) 363.3171
Fax: (416) 363.5963

Les Éditions La Liberté Inc.
3020 Chemin Sainte-Foy
Sainte-Foy, PQ G1X 3V6 Tel. (418) 658.3763
Fax: (418) 658.3763

Federal Publications Inc.
165 University Avenue, Suite 701
Toronto, ON M5H 3B8   Tel. (416) 860.1611
Fax: (416) 860.1608

Les Publications Fédérales
1185 Université
Montréal, QC H3B 3A7 Tel. (514) 954.1633
Fax: (514) 954.1635

CHINA – CHINE
Book Dept., China National Publications
Import and Export Corporation (CNPIEC)
16 Gongti E. Road, Chaoyang District
Beijing 100020 Tel. (10) 6506-6688 Ext. 8402
(10) 6506-3101

CHINESE TAIPEI – TAIPEI CHINOIS
Good Faith Worldwide Int'l. Co. Ltd.
9th Floor, No. 118, Sec. 2
Chung Hsiao E. Road
Taipei   Tel. (02) 391.7396/391.7397
Fax: (02) 394.9176

**CZECH REPUBLIC –
RÉPUBLIQUE TCHÈQUE**
National Information Centre
NIS – prodejna
Konviktská 5
Praha 1 – 113 57   Tel. (02) 24.23.09.07
Fax: (02) 24.22.94.33
E-mail: nkposp@dec.niz.cz
Internet: http://www.nis.cz

DENMARK – DANEMARK
Munksgaard Book and Subscription Service
35, Nørre Søgade, P.O. Box 2148
DK-1016 København K   Tel. (33) 12.85.70
Fax: (33) 12.93.87

J. H. Schultz Information A/S,
Herstedvang 12,
DK – 2620 Albertslung   Tel. 43 63 23 00
Fax: 43 63 19 69
Internet: s-info@inet.uni-c.dk

EGYPT – ÉGYPTE
The Middle East Observer
41 Sherif Street
Cairo   Tel. (2) 392.6919
Fax: (2) 360.6804

FINLAND – FINLANDE
Akateeminen Kirjakauppa
Keskuskatu 1, P.O. Box 128
00100 Helsinki

Subscription Services/Agence d'abonnements :
P.O. Box 23
00100 Helsinki   Tel. (358) 9.121.4403
Fax: (358) 9.121.4450

*FRANCE
OECD/OCDE
Mail Orders/Commandes par correspondance :
2, rue André-Pascal
75775 Paris Cedex 16 Tel. 33 (0)1.45.24.82.00
Fax: 33 (0)1.49.10.42.76
Telex: 640048 OCDE
Internet: Compte.PUBSINQ@oecd.org

Orders via Minitel, France only/
Commandes par Minitel, France
exclusivement : 36 15 OCDE

OECD Bookshop/Librairie de l'OCDE :
33, rue Octave-Feuillet
75016 Paris   Tel. 33 (0)1.45.24.81.81
33 (0)1.45.24.81.67

Dawson
B.P. 40
91121 Palaiseau Cedex   Tel. 01.89.10.47.00
Fax: 01.64.54.83.26

Documentation Française
29, quai Voltaire
75007 Paris   Tel. 01.40.15.70.00

Economica
49, rue Héricart
75015 Paris   Tel. 01.45.78.12.92
Fax: 01.45.75.05.67

Gibert Jeune (Droit-Économie)
6, place Saint-Michel
75006 Paris   Tel. 01.43.25.91.19

Librairie du Commerce International
10, avenue d'Iéna
75016 Paris   Tel. 01.40.73.34.60

Librairie Dunod
Université Paris-Dauphine
Place du Maréchal-de-Lattre-de-Tassigny
75016 Paris   Tel. 01.44.05.40.13

Librairie Lavoisier
11, rue Lavoisier
75008 Paris   Tel. 01.42.65.39.95

Librairie des Sciences Politiques
30, rue Saint-Guillaume
75007 Paris   Tel. 01.45.48.36.02

P.U.F.
49, boulevard Saint-Michel
75005 Paris   Tel. 01.43.25.83.40

Librairie de l'Université
12a, rue Nazareth
13100 Aix-en-Provence Tel. 04.42.26.18.08

Documentation Française
165, rue Garibaldi
69003 Lyon   Tel. 04.78.63.32.23

Librairie Decitre
29, place Bellecour
69002 Lyon   Tel. 04.72.40.54.54

Librairie Sauramps
Le Triangle
34967 Montpellier Cedex 2 Tel. 04.67.58.85.15
Fax: 04.67.58.27.36

A la Sorbonne Actual
23, rue de l'Hôtel-des-Postes
06000 Nice   Tel. 04.93.13.77.75
Fax: 04.93.80.75.69

GERMANY – ALLEMAGNE
OECD Bonn Centre
August-Bebel-Allee 6
D-53175 Bonn   Tel. (0228) 959.120
Fax: (0228) 959.12.17

GREECE – GRÈCE
Librairie Kauffmann
Stadiou 28
10564 Athens   Tel. (01) 32.55.321
Fax: (01) 32.30.320

HONG-KONG
Swindon Book Co. Ltd.
Astoria Bldg. 3F
34 Ashley Road, Tsimshatsui
Kowloon, Hong Kong   Tel. 2376.2062
Fax: 2376.0685

HUNGARY – HONGRIE
Euro Info Service
Margitsziget, Európa Ház
1138 Budapest   Tel. (1) 111.60.61
Fax: (1) 302.50.35
E-mail: euroinfo@mail.matav.hu
Internet: http://www.euroinfo.hu//index.html

ICELAND – ISLANDE
Mál og Menning
Laugavegi 18, Pósthólf 392
121 Reykjavik   Tel. (1) 552.4240
Fax: (1) 562.3523

INDIA – INDE
Oxford Book and Stationery Co.
Scindia House
New Delhi 110001   Tel. (11) 331.5896/5308
Fax. (11) 332.2639
E-mail: oxford.publ@axcess.net.in

17 Park Street
Calcutta 700016   Tel. 240832

INDONESIA – INDONÉSIE
Pdii-Lipi
P.O. Box 4298
Jakarta 12042   Tel. (21) 573.34.67
Fax: (21) 573.34.67

IRELAND – IRLANDE
Government Supplies Agency
Publications Section
4/5 Harcourt Road
Dublin 2   Tel. 661.31.11
Fax: 475.27.60

ISRAEL – ISRAËL
Praedicta
5 Shatner Street
P.O. Box 34030
Jerusalem 91430   Tel. (2) 652.84.90/1/2
Fax: (2) 652.84.93

R.O.Y. International
P.O. Box 13056
Tel Aviv 61130   Tel. (3) 546 1423
Fax: (3) 546 1442
E mail: royil@netvision.net.il

Palestinian Authority/Middle East:
INDEX Information Services
P.O.B. 19502
Jerusalem   Tel. (2) 627.16.34
Fax: (2) 627.12.19

ITALY – ITALIE
Libreria Commissionaria Sansoni
Via Duca di Calabria, 1/1
50125 Firenze   Tel. (055) 64.54.15
Fax: (055) 64.12.57
E-mail: licosa@ftbcc.it

Via Bartolini 29
20155 Milano   Tel. (02) 36.50.83

Editrice e Libreria Herder
Piazza Montecitorio 120
00186 Roma   Tel. 679.46.28
Fax: 678.47.51

Libreria Hoepli
Via Hoepli 5
20121 Milano   Tel. (02) 86.54.46
                       Fax: (02) 805.28.86

Libreria Scientifica
Dott. Lucio de Biasio 'Aeiou'
Via Coronelli, 6
20146 Milano   Tel. (02) 48.95.45.52
                       Fax: (02) 48.95.45.48

JAPAN – JAPON
OECD Tokyo Centre
Landic Akasaka Building
2-3-4 Akasaka, Minato-ku
Tokyo 107   Tel. (81.3) 3586.2016
                       Fax: (81.3) 3584.7929

KOREA – CORÉE
Kyobo Book Centre Co. Ltd.
P.O. Box 1658, Kwang Hwa Moon
Seoul   Tel. 730.78.91
                       Fax: 735.00.30

MALAYSIA – MALAISIE
University of Malaya Bookshop
University of Malaya
P.O. Box 1127, Jalan Pantai Baru
59700 Kuala Lumpur
Malaysia   Tel. 756.5000/756.5425
                       Fax: 756.3246

MEXICO – MEXIQUE
OECD Mexico Centre
Edificio INFOTEC
Av. San Fernando no. 37
Col. Toriello Guerra
Tlalpan C.P. 14050
Mexico D.F.   Tel. (525) 528.10.38
                       Fax: (525) 606.13.07
E-mail: ocde@rtn.net.mx

NETHERLANDS – PAYS-BAS
SDU Uitgeverij Plantijnstraat
Externe Fondsen
Postbus 20014
2500 EA's-Gravenhage   Tel. (070) 37.89.880
Voor bestellingen: Fax: (070) 34.75.778

Subscription Agency/Agence d'abonnements :
SWETS & ZEITLINGER BV
Heereweg 347B
P.O. Box 830
2160 SZ Lisse   Tel. 252.435.111
                       Fax: 252.415.888

**NEW ZEALAND –
NOUVELLE-ZÉLANDE**
GPLegislation Services
P.O. Box 12418
Thorndon, Wellington   Tel. (04) 496.5655
                       Fax: (04) 496.5698

NORWAY – NORVÈGE
NIC INFO A/S
Ostensjoveien 18
P.O. Box 6512 Etterstad
0606 Oslo   Tel. (22) 97.45.00
                       Fax: (22) 97.45.45

PAKISTAN
Mirza Book Agency
65 Shahrah Quaid-E-Azam
Lahore 54000   Tel. (42) 735.36.01
                       Fax: (42) 576.37.14

PHILIPPINE – PHILIPPINS
International Booksource Center Inc.
Rm 179/920 Cityland 10 Condo Tower 2
HV dela Costa Ext cor Valero St.
Makati Metro Manila   Tel. (632) 817 9676
                       Fax: (632) 817 1741

POLAND – POLOGNE
Ars Polona
00-950 Warszawa
Krakowskie Prezdmiescie 7 Tel. (22) 264760
                       Fax: (22) 265334

PORTUGAL
Livraria Portugal
Rua do Carmo 70-74
Apart. 2681
1200 Lisboa   Tel. (01) 347.49.82/5
                       Fax: (01) 347.02.64

SINGAPORE – SINGAPOUR
Ashgate Publishing
Asia Pacific Pte. Ltd
Golden Wheel Building, 04-03
41, Kallang Pudding Road
Singapore 349316   Tel. 741.5166
                       Fax: 742.9356

SPAIN – ESPAGNE
Mundi-Prensa Libros S.A.
Castelló 37, Apartado 1223
Madrid 28001   Tel. (91) 431.33.99
                       Fax: (91) 575.39.98
E-mail: mundiprensa@tsai.es
Internet: http://www.mundiprensa.es

Mundi-Prensa Barcelona
Consell de Cent No. 391
08009 – Barcelona   Tel. (93) 488.34.92
                       Fax: (93) 487.76.59

Libreria de la Generalitat
Palau Moja
Rambla dels Estudis, 118
08002 – Barcelona
              (Suscripciones) Tel. (93) 318.80.12
              (Publicaciones) Tel. (93) 302.67.23
                       Fax: (93) 412.18.54

SRI LANKA
Centre for Policy Research
c/o Colombo Agencies Ltd.
No. 300-304, Galle Road
Colombo 3   Tel. (1) 574240, 573551-2
                       Fax: (1) 575394, 510711

SWEDEN – SUÈDE
CE Fritzes AB
S–106 47 Stockholm   Tel. (08) 690.90.90
                       Fax: (08) 20.50.21

For electronic publications only/
Publications électroniques seulement
STATISTICS SWEDEN
Informationsservice
S–115 81 Stockholm   Tel. 8 783 5066
                       Fax: 8 783 4045

Subscription Agency/Agence d'abonnements :
Wennergren-Williams Info AB
P.O. Box 1305
171 25 Solna   Tel. (08) 705.97.50
                       Fax: (08) 27.00.71

Liber distribution
Internatinal organizations
Fagerstagatan 21
S-163 52 Spanga

SWITZERLAND – SUISSE
Maditec S.A. (Books and Periodicals/Livres
et périodiques)
Chemin des Palettes 4
Case postale 266
1020 Renens VD 1   Tel. (021) 635.08.65
                       Fax: (021) 635.07.80

Librairie Payot S.A.
4, place Pépinet
CP 3212
1002 Lausanne   Tel. (021) 320.25.11
                       Fax: (021) 320.25.14

Librairie Unilivres
6, rue de Candolle
1205 Genève   Tel. (022) 320.26.23
                       Fax: (022) 329.73.18

Subscription Agency/Agence d'abonnements :
Dynapresse Marketing S.A.
38, avenue Vibert
1227 Carouge   Tel. (022) 308.08.70
                       Fax: (022) 308.07.99

See also – Voir aussi :
OECD Bonn Centre
August-Bebel-Allee 6
D-53175 Bonn (Germany) Tel. (0228) 959.120
                       Fax: (0228) 959.12.17

THAILAND – THAÏLANDE
Suksit Siam Co. Ltd.
113, 115 Fuang Nakhon Rd.
Opp. Wat Rajbopith
Bangkok 10200   Tel. (662) 225.9531/2
                       Fax: (662) 222.5188

**TRINIDAD & TOBAGO, CARIBBEAN
TRINITÉ-ET-TOBAGO, CARAÏBES**
Systematics Studies Limited
9 Watts Street
Curepe
Trinidad & Tobago, W.I. Tel. (1809) 645.3475
                       Fax: (1809) 662.5654
E-mail: tobe@trinidad.net

TUNISIA – TUNISIE
Grande Librairie Spécialisée
Fendri Ali
Avenue Haffouz Imm El-Intilaka
Bloc B 1 Sfax 3000   Tel. (216-4) 296 855
                       Fax: (216-4) 298.270

TURKEY – TURQUIE
Kültür Yayinlari Is-Türk Ltd.
Atatürk Bulvari No. 191/Kat 13
06684 Kavaklidere/Ankara
                       Tel. (312) 428.11.40 Ext. 2458
                       Fax : (312) 417.24.90

Dolmabahce Cad. No. 29
Besiktas/Istanbul   Tel. (212) 260 7188

UNITED KINGDOM – ROYAUME-UNI
The Stationery Office Ltd.
Postal orders only:
P.O. Box 276, London SW8 5DT
Gen. enquiries   Tel. (171) 873 0011
                       Fax: (171) 873 8463

The Stationery Office Ltd.
Postal orders only:
49 High Holborn, London WC1V 6HB
Branches at: Belfast, Birmingham, Bristol,
Edinburgh, Manchester

UNITED STATES – ÉTATS-UNIS
OECD Washington Center
2001 L Street N.W., Suite 650
Washington, D.C. 20036-4922
                       Tel. (202) 785.6323
                       Fax: (202) 785.0350
Internet: washcont@oecd.org

Subscriptions to OECD periodicals may also
be placed through main subscription agencies.

Les abonnements aux publications périodiques
de l'OCDE peuvent être souscrits auprès des
principales agences d'abonnement.

Orders and inquiries from countries where Dis-
tributors have not yet been appointed should be
sent to: OECD Publications, 2, rue André-Pascal, 75775 Paris Cedex 16, France.

Les commandes provenant de pays où l'OCDE
n'a pas encore désigné de distributeur peuvent
être adressées aux Éditions de l'OCDE, 2, rue
André-Pascal, 75775 Paris Cedex 16, France.

12-1996

OECD PUBLICATIONS, 2, rue André-Pascal, 75775 PARIS CEDEX 16
PRINTED IN FRANCE
(96 97 06 1 P) ISBN 92-64-15601-1 – No. 49675 1997